The Secret to
HOLY SPIRIT
AUTHORITY

The Secret to
HOLY SPIRIT
AUTHORITY

In the Power of the Spirit

DAVID CHARLES CRALEY

authorHOUSE®

AuthorHouse™
1663 Liberty Drive
Bloomington, IN 47403
www.authorhouse.com
Phone: 1-800-839-8640

Cover photo: NASA. Used by permission.

First published by AuthorHouse   10/29/2011

ISBN: 978-1-4670-4111-9 (sc)
ISBN: 978-1-4670-4109-6 (ebk)

Printed in the United States of America

This book is printed on acid-free paper.

CONTENTS

"Truly, truly, I say to you,
whoever believes in me
will also do the works that I do;
and greater works than these will he do,
because I am going to the Father.
Whatever you ask in my name,
this I will do,
that the Father may be glorified in the Son.
If you ask me anything in my name,
I will do it."

JOHN 14:12-14, ESV

PREFACE

"In the power of the Spirit," Jesus Christ opened the eyes of the blind, made the lame to walk, healed the sick, cast out demons, raised the dead, and set the captives free at every opportunity. Moreover, He made an astounding promise to His disciples: "Most assuredly, I say to you, he who believes in Me, the works that I do he will do also; and greater works than these he will do, because I go to My Father. And whatever you ask in My name, that I will do, that the Father may be glorified in the Son. If you ask anything in My name, I will do it" [John 14:12-14, NKJV].

Alas, down through the centuries since Jesus walked this earth, much misunderstanding and confusion— issuing in unbelief—has clouded the minds of sincere followers of Christ regarding such seeming mysteries as the baptism in holy spirit, the *pneumatikos* [things] of the spirit including speaking in tongues, the "anointing" of the Lord, "transformation" by the renewal of the mind, praying "without ceasing," walking by the spirit, as well as the working of miracles and believing faith for gifts of healing. Nevertheless, if a faithful believer in Christ desires to rise up in faith to *take the Lord at His word*—"If you ask anything in My name, I will do it"—and then honestly expect the Lord to work in him "in the power of the Spirit" to accomplish His will, then surely he must gain a progressive understanding of God's word regarding every one of these spiritual arenas and their practical application.

The Secret to Holy Spirit Authority: In the Power of the Spirit is a study in biblical keys. Especially, it is for believers in Jesus Christ who have longed for and yet remain unsatisfied with God's promise of the fullness of the power and authority of "Christ in you." As well, those who have not received Jesus Christ as their Lord and Savior and may even have doubted His resurrection and living reality—but *hoped*—might very well come face to face with Him in the pages of this book.

This study is not meant to be the last word on these subjects. However, if the Lord's promise to His disciples is true—that we can and should be doing the works that He did in His earthly ministry—and greater works than these, then there must be answers in the word of God, there must be keys to help us understand *how*. To be sure, the secret to holy spirit authority is a secret not because God is keeping it to Himself. It's a secret because most Christians have not understood and therefore have not believed the great keys and principles in the word of God which unlock "the mystery of God, both of the Father and of Christ, in whom are hidden all the treasures of knowledge and wisdom" [Colossians 2:2b,3 NKJV].

Herein are those keys.

ONE

"In the power of the Spirit"

The Gospel of Luke tells us that, after spending forty days in the wilderness "being tempted by the devil," Jesus returned "in the power of the Spirit to Galilee . . . ." Coming to Nazareth where He had been brought up, "as His custom was, He went into the synagogue on the Sabbath day, and stood up to read. And He was handed the book [scroll] of the prophet Isaiah. And when He had opened the book, He found the place where it was written:

> The Spirit of the Lord is upon Me,
> because He has anointed Me to preach
> the gospel to the poor;
> He has sent Me to heal the brokenhearted,
> to proclaim liberty to the captives
> and recovery of sight to the blind,
> to set at liberty those who are oppressed;
> to proclaim the acceptable year of the Lord.

Then He closed the book, and gave it back to the attendant and sat down. And the eyes of all who were in the synagogue were fixed on Him. And He began to say to them, 'Today this scripture is fulfilled in your hearing'" [Luke 4:14-21, NKJV].

Thus began the remarkable healing and deliverance ministry of Jesus of Nazareth, son of man and Son of God. The Bible tells us that Jesus returned to Galilee "in the power of the Spirit." In the Greek text of the New Testament from which we get our English translations, the word for "power" in Luke 4:14, as well as in numerous other scriptures, is *dunamis*. According to Thayer's Lexicon of the Greek New

Testament, *dunamis* means "strength, ability, power; inherent power, power residing in a thing by virtue of its nature." The "nature" of Jesus' power was the spirit that was upon Him.

Where did Jesus get this "inherent power"? Luke 3:16 says that while John the Baptist was baptizing the people in the Jordan River, he prophesied, saying, "I indeed baptize you with water; but One mightier than I is coming, whose sandal strap I am not worthy to loose. He will baptize you with the Holy Spirit and with fire . . . . When all the people were baptized, it came to pass that Jesus also was baptized; and while He prayed, the heaven was opened. And the Holy Spirit descended in bodily form upon Him, and a voice came from heaven which said, 'You are My beloved Son; in You I am well pleased'" [vss. 21,22, NKJV].

Jesus received *dunamis*—"strength, inherent power"—dynamic ability by means of the spirit upon Him, given to Him by His Heavenly Father, who is *the* Holy Spirit. Soon after His baptism in the spirit, "Jesus, being filled with the Holy Spirit, returned from the Jordan and was led by the Spirit into the wilderness, being tempted for forty days by the devil" [Luke 4:1,2, NKJV]. This period of forty days was the Lord's accelerated "proving ground" in learning to "walk by the spirit," that is, in learning to perceive the voice of His Heavenly Father communicating with Him via the spirit. In the wilderness He was "tempted" [*peirazo*-"tried, tested, proved"] by his experiences in dealing with the devil. Jesus was prepared. Since He was a boy He had been reading, studying, memorizing the Old Testament Scriptures—beginning with the time when He was twelve years old and His parents "found Him in the temple [in Jerusalem], sitting in the midst of the teachers, both listening to them and asking them questions. And all who heard Him were astonished with His understanding and answers. So when they saw Him, they were amazed; and His mother said to Him, 'Son, why have you done this to us? Look, your father and I have sought you anxiously.' And He said to them, 'Why did you seek Me? Did you not know that I must be about My Father's business?' But they did not understand the statement that He spoke to them . . . Then He went down with them and came to Nazareth, and was subject to them, but His mother kept all these things in her heart. And Jesus increased in wisdom and stature, and in favor with God and men" [Luke 2:46-50, NKJV].

It's important to understand that in His forty days of being tested, tried, and proven in the wilderness, Jesus was able to stand against the temptations and schemes of the devil because He had prepared Himself for this testing all of His young life by studying the Scriptures so that the spirit—working in Him—brought to His remembrance what the Scriptures said about every situation the devil tried to draw Him into. Jesus replied, "It is written, 'Man shall not live by bread alone, but by every word of God' . . . It is written . . . It is written" [Luke 4:4, etc., NKJV].

". . . in the power of the spirit . . ."

Looking back upon his own astonishing experiences "in training" with the Lord, the apostle Peter on the Day of Pentecost, when the Lord poured out the gift of holy spirit for the first time, said to the people: "Men of Israel, hear these words: Jesus of Nazareth, a Man attested by God to you by miracles, wonders, and signs which God did through Him in your midst, as you yourselves know—" [Acts 2:22, NKJV]. And again in Acts 10:38 Peter testifies to the Lord's ministry: ". . . how God anointed Jesus of Nazareth with the Holy Spirit and with power [*dunamis*], who went about doing good and healing all who were oppressed by the devil, for God was with Him." Thus the Scriptures make it clear that Jesus exercised remarkable power—*dunamis*—"strength, ability, inherent power." After His resurrection from the dead, Jesus tells His disciples: "All authority [*exousia*-"exercised power, ability, strength, liberty"] has been given to me in heaven and on earth" [Matthew 28:18, NKJV]. And in John 17:1b and 2 He prays: "Father, the hour has come. Glorify Your Son that Your Son may also glorify You, as You have given Him authority [*exousia*] over all flesh, that He should give eternal life to as many as you have given Him." Clearly this power and authority "in heaven and on earth" came from His Heavenly Father via the spirit after He was baptized by John in the Jordan when the heaven opened and the spirit like a dove descended upon Him.

". . . heal the brokenhearted . . ."

Throughout His short ministry on earth, Jesus exercised this dynamic power and authority to "heal the brokenhearted, to proclaim liberty to the captives and recovery of sight to the blind, to set at liberty those that are oppressed . . . ." Mark chapter 5 tells of "a certain woman who had a flow of blood for twelve years," and who "had suffered many things from many physicians" and "had spent all that she had and was no better but rather grew worse." As the story progresses, "When she heard about Jesus, she came behind Him in the crowd and touched His garment. For she said, 'If only I may touch His clothes, I will be made well.' Immediately the fountain of her blood was dried up, and she felt in her body that she was healed of her affliction. And Jesus, immediately knowing in Himself that power [*dunamis*] had gone out of Him, turned around in the crowd and said, 'Who touched My clothes?'" [Mark 5:25-30, NKJV]. Regarding this same incident, Luke 8:46 says: "But Jesus said, 'Somebody touched Me, for I perceived [*ginosko*-"came to know, understood, felt"] power [*dunamis*] going out from Me'" [NKJV]. Whether Jesus had a physical sensation of power going out from Him, or He perceived it spiritually, He knew and understood what had occurred. Some versions of the Bible translate *dunamis* as "virtue" in these verses. Jesus felt inherent strength and ability given to Him by God by means of His baptism in the spirit go out of Him to heal the woman of her infirmity.

At every opportunity Jesus sought to "set at liberty those who (were) oppressed." Luke 6:17-19 says: ". . . a great multitude from all Judea and Jerusalem, and from the seacoast of Tyre and Sidon, . . . came to hear Him and be healed of their diseases, as well as those who were tormented with unclean spirits. And they were healed. And the whole multitude sought to touch Him, for power [*dunamis*] went out from Him and healed them all" [NKJV].

Jesus not only exercised great power and authority in doing His Father's will, He also exercised the privilege of giving it to whomever He chose. Luke 9 says: "Then He called His twelve disciples together and gave them power [*dunamis*] and authority [*exousia*] over all demons, and to cure diseases. He sent them to preach the kingdom of God and to heal the sick . . . So they departed and went through the towns, preaching the gospel and healing everywhere" [Luke 9:1,2,6, NKJV]. As well, in Luke 10 "the Lord appointed seventy others also, and sent them two by two before His face into every city and place where He Himself was about to go. Then He said to them, 'He who hears you hears Me, he who rejects you rejects Me, and he who rejects Me rejects Him who sent Me.' Then the seventy returned with joy, saying, 'Lord, even the demons are subject to us in Your name.' And He said to them, 'I saw Satan fall like lightning from heaven. Behold, I give you the authority [*exousia*] to trample on serpents and scorpions, and over all the power of the enemy, and nothing shall by any means hurt you. Nevertheless do not rejoice in this, that the serpents are subject to you, but rather rejoice because your names are written in heaven'" [Luke 10:1,16,17-20, NKJV].

It's a remarkable truth that this spiritual power and authority exercised by Jesus throughout His earthly ministry did not cease with His ascension into heaven to sit down at the right hand of the throne of God. Prior to His ascension Jesus promised His disciples: "Thus it is written and thus it was necessary for the Christ to suffer and to rise from the dead the third day, and that repentance and remission of sins should be preached in His name to all nations, beginning in Jerusalem. And you are witnesses of these things. Behold, I send the Promise of My Father upon you; but tarry in the city of Jerusalem until you are endued with power [*dunamis*] from on high" [Luke 24:46-49, NKJV]. Inherent in the Lord's promise that His disciples would be "endued" [*endyo*-"arrayed, clothed"] with "power from on high" was His exclamation in John 14:12-14: "Most assuredly, I say to you, he who believes in Me, the works that I do he will do also; and greater works than these he will do, because I go to My Father. And whatever you ask in My name, that I will do that the Father may be glorified in the Son. If you ask anything in My name, I will do it" [NKJV].

"... the mystery of God ..."

In Colossians chapter 2, the apostle Paul prays for the believers in Laodicea "and for as many as have not seen my face in the flesh, that their hearts may be encouraged, being knit together in love, and attaining to all riches of the full assurance of understanding, to the knowledge of the mystery of God, both of the Father and of Christ, in whom are hidden all the treasures of wisdom and knowledge" [Colossians 2:1b,2,3, NKJV]. This "mystery of God"—*mysterion* in the Greek text—which Paul, by inspiration (in-spirit action) from God prays that all believers might attain unto—"all riches of the full assurance of understanding"— is, according to Strong's Lexicon, "a hidden or secret thing," "a secret," "a hidden purpose or counsel," and "confided only to the initiated and not to ordinary mortals." Once an "ordinary mortal" (such as you or I) hears "the word of truth, the gospel of your salvation" [Ephesians 1:13a, NKJV] and "confesses with (his) mouth the Lord Jesus and believes in (his) heart that God has raised Him from the dead, (he is) saved" [sozo-"rescued from danger or destruction"] [Romans 10:9, NKJV]. At that time he is "sealed with the Holy Spirit of promise" [Ephesians 1:13b] and "endued with power [dunamis] from on high" [Luke 24:49b] which is "the Promise of the Father" [Luke 24:49a] which is to be "baptized with the Holy Spirit" [Acts 1:5, NKJV]. Thereupon the new believer in Christ is encouraged to embark upon a "mystery tour" of the Holy Scriptures wherein day by day is revealed to his understanding "the mystery of God" which God makes known only to those faithful believers who determine to become true disciples of the Lord Jesus Christ with all integrity of heart and willingness to obey the Lord's commandment to search the Scriptures daily in order, step by step, to attain unto "all riches of the full assurance of understanding, to the knowledge of the mystery of God, both of the Father and of Christ, in whom are hidden all the treasures of wisdom and knowledge." But let there be no mystery about this one thing: the records of healing and deliverance in the four Gospels and in the Acts of the Apostles are profound *instructive lessons* for teachable believers. This truth is pursued in chapters 10-12. "He who has ears to hear, let him hear!" [Matthew 11:15, NKJV].

God assures us that "All Scripture is given by inspiration of God, and is profitable for doctrine, for reproof, for correction, for instruction in righteousness, that the man of God may be complete, thoroughly equipped for every good work" [2 Timothy 3:16,17, NKJV]. The phrase "given by inspiration of God" is one word in the Greek text—*theopneustos,* which means "God-breathed." Here we have a figure of speech emphasizing the truth that "All Scripture is God-breathed . . . ." As well, Peter says: "Knowing this first, that no prophecy [either forth telling or foretelling] of Scripture is of any private interpretation [or origin], for prophecy never came by the will of man, but holy men of God spoke as they were moved by the Holy Spirit" [2 Peter 1:20,21, NKJV]. The "God-breathed" records of healing and deliverance in the Scriptures unlock the keys and reveal the step by step guidelines and principles that enable faithful believers to tap the limitless resources of holy spirit power and authority.

Jesus promised His disciples that we can and should do the works that He did—and greater, for the glory of God and the deliverance of His people. With revolutionary prophetic insight, the following chapters in this book unfold to the reader *how* Jesus did it, *how* His disciples did it, and *how* Christians today can rise up spiritually "to heal the brokenhearted, to proclaim liberty to the captives and recovery of sight to the blind," and "to set at liberty those who are oppressed."

Summary
"In the power of the Spirit"

At every opportunity Jesus sought to "set at liberty those who were oppressed."

Verse to Remember: "Most assuredly, I say to you, he who believes in Me the works that I do he will do also; and greater works than these he will do, because I go to My Father" [John 14:12, NKJV].

Question to ask Myself: Have I ever longed to walk in the power and authority of Jesus Christ "to set at liberty those who are oppressed"?

Exercise: Read Luke 4:18 again. Carefully consider each of the Lord's declarations. Can I apply any of these purposes in my own life and ministry, or were they only for Jesus and His?

Note: In most versions of the Bible, the words "Holy Spirit" are capitalized when referring both to God and to His gift. This can only be confusing to the reader. In the text of this book, however, in order to differentiate between God and His gift given to every Christian believer, Holy Spirit is capitalized when referring to God and in lower case when referring to God's gift of holy spirit. In direct quotes from various versions of the Bible, capitalization determined by the translators has been left intact.

TWO

"Power from on high"

"**T**arry in the City of Jerusalem until you are endued [*endyo*-"clothed, arrayed"] with power [*dunamis*-"inherent power, strength"] from on high," Jesus told His disciples. And immediately prior to His ascension, He commands them to ". . . wait for the Promise of the Father, 'which,' He said, 'you have heard from Me; for John truly baptized with water, but you shall be baptized with the Holy Spirit not many days from now'" [Acts 1:4b,5, NKJV]. He continued: ". . . you shall receive [*lambano*-"take up, lay hold of, receive evidence of"] power [*dunamis*] when the Holy Spirit has come upon you; and you shall be witnesses unto Me in Jerusalem, and in all Judea and Samaria, and to the end of the earth" [v. 8].

What was "the Promise of the Father" of which Jesus spoke? It must be understood that Jesus knew nothing of the Administration of God's Grace which God would usher in beginning on the Day of Pentecost. This new dispensation of God was a "mystery which," Colossians 1:26 says, "has been hidden from ages and from generations, but now [by means of the Lord's revelation to Paul] has been revealed to His saints" [NKJV]. Jesus knew only that "the Promise of the Father" was for Israel in the future Millennial Kingdom. He could have anticipated that this kingdom would come to pass after His resurrection. In John 14 Jesus says, "If you love me, keep My commandments. And I will pray the Father, and He will give you another Helper [some versions of the Bible read "Counselor," "Advocate," "Comforter"] that He may abide with you forever—the Spirit of truth, whom the world cannot receive because it neither sees Him nor knows Him; but you know Him, for He dwells with you and will be in you. I will not leave you orphans; I will come to you. A little while longer and the world will see Me no more, but you will see Me. Because I live, you will live also. At that day you will know that I am in My Father, and you in Me, and I in you" [John 14:13-20, NKJV]. Jesus promises His disciples that He will by no means leave them "orphans," but that He will pray to His Father to send them "the Spirit of truth"—the "Helper," "Counselor," "Comforter"—"for He dwells with you and will be in you" to strengthen, teach, guide, and *enable* them to do the works that He did because "I go to the Father."

"The Promise of the Father," which Ezekiel and Isaiah prophesied regarding Israel in the future Millennial Kingdom, actually came to pass early, by God's grace, at Pentecost. The apostles did not know that it was the advent of a new age "kept secret since the world began" but later revealed by the Lord to Paul [Colossians 1:26; 1 Corinthians 2:7,8]. Following the election of Matthias to replace Judas, the apostles were "all with one accord in one place [in the temple]. And suddenly there came a sound from heaven, as of a rushing mighty wind, and it filled the whole house where they were sitting. Then there appeared to them divided tongues, as of fire, and one sat upon each of them. And they were all filled [*pletho*-"filled to overflowing"] with the Holy Spirit and began to speak with other tongues as the Spirit gave them utterance" [Acts 2:1b-4]. Shortly thereafter in perhaps the greatest sermon ever recorded, Peter tells the people: "Men of Israel, hear these words: Jesus of Nazareth, a Man attested by God to you by miracles, wonders, and signs which God did through Him, in your midst, as you yourselves also know—Him being delivered by the determined purpose and foreknowledge of God, you have taken by lawless hands, have crucified, and have put to death; whom God raised up, having loosed the pains of death, because it was not possible that He should be held by it . . . . This Jesus God has raised up, of which we are all witnesses. Therefore being exalted to the right hand of God, and having received from the Father the promise of the Holy Spirit, He poured out this which you now see and hear" [Acts 2:22-24, 32,33, NKJV].

Peter's boldness on the Day of Pentecost is remarkable. Up until that time, Peter had been a vacillating disciple of Jesus, having denied Him three times prior to His trial and crucifixion. John 20:19 informs us that even after the Lord's resurrection, the disciples had shut themselves up behind locked doors "for fear of the Jews." They were deathly afraid that what had happened to Jesus on the cross would also happen to them. But on the Day of Pentecost, Peter stood beforethe assembled throng in the public square in Jerusalem and, with astonishing new boldness and understanding, proclaimed Jesus—Him crucified by their "lawless hands"—but raised from the dead by the power of God. What changed Peter? Clearly it was the baptism in holy spirit—"the Promise of the Father"—strengthening him, giving him understanding and wisdom. From that day forward, as recorded throughout the Book of Acts, Peter, James, John, and the other disciples of Jesus manifested tremendous boldness and purpose, accompanied by God's power and authority—holy spirit working in them as they preached the gospel of Jesus Christ in Jerusalem and throughout Judea and Samaria.

Acts chapter 3 tells how Peter healed "a certain man lame from his mother's womb" at the Beautiful Gate of the temple so that the man, "leaping up, stood and walked and entered the temple with them— walking, leaping, and praising God" [vss. 2,8, NKJV]. The ensuing commotion got Peter and John in trouble so that the authorities put them in custody until the next day until the high priest and his consorts brought them forth and demanded: "By what power or by what name have you done this? Then Peter, filled with the Holy Spirit, said to them, 'Rulers of the people and elders of Israel: If we this day are judged for a good deed done to a helpless man, by what means he has been made well, let it be known to you all, and to all the people of Israel, that by the name of Jesus Christ of Nazareth, whom you crucified, whom God raised from the dead, by Him this man stands here before you whole'" [Acts 4:7-10, NKJV].

"Filled with the Holy Spirit," Peter boldly proclaims Christ to the high priest and the assembly. Later, being let go, "they went to their own companions and reported all that the chief priests and elders had said to them" [v. 23]. "And when they had prayed, the place where they were assembled together was shaken; and and they were all filled with the Holy Spirit, and they spoke the word of God with boldness . . . And with great power [*dunamis*] the apostles gave witness to the resurrection of the Lord Jesus. And great grace was upon them all" [vss. 31, 33, NKJV]. These dramatic events in Acts 4 are pivotal to the growth of the early Church and are illuminating to our study of the secret to holy spirit authority, as we will see in chapter 11.

"Stephen, full of faith and power"

As the history of the rise and expansion of the Christian Church unfolds in the Book of Acts, we find Stephen—not an apostle, but "full of faith and power" [dunamis]—doing "great wonders and signs among the people" [Acts 6:8, NKJV]. And in Acts 10, Peter preaches to the household of Cornelius "how God anointed Jesus of Nazareth with the Holy Spirit and with power [dunamis], who went about doing good and healing all who were oppressed by the devil, for God was with Him" [v. 38]. The story continues: "While Peter was still speaking these words, the Holy Spirit fell upon all those who heard the word. And those of the circumcision who believed were astonished, as many as came with Peter, because the gift of the Holy Sprit had been poured out on the Gentiles also. For they heard them speak with tongues and magnify God" [vss. 44-46, NKJV].

Acts chapter 9 brings Saul of Tarsus on the scene. On the road to Damascus Saul meets the Lord Jesus in a blinding light and is ministered to by a disciple named Ananias: "And Ananias went his way, and entered the house; and laying his hands on him he said, 'Brother Saul, the Lord Jesus, who appeared to you on the road as you came, has sent me that you may receive your sight and be filled [pletho-"filled to overflowing"] with the Holy Spirit'" [Acts 9:17, NKJV]. In Romans 15 Paul reminds his friends how the Lord worked in his ministry: "For I will not dare to speak of any of those things which Christ has not accomplished through me, in word and deed, to make the Gentiles obedient—in mighty signs and wonders, by the power [dunamis] of the Spirit of God, so that from Jerusalem and round about to Illyricum I have fully preached the gospel of Christ" [vss. 18,19, NKJV]. Moreover, he reminds the Corinthians that his speech and his preaching in their midst "were not with persuasive words of human wisdom, but in demonstration [apodakses-"showing forth, proof"] of the Spirit and of power [dunamis], that your faith should not be in the wisdom of men but in the power [dunamis] of God" [1 Corinthians 2:4,5, NKJV]. Again he assures them: ". . . I will come to you shortly, if the Lord wills, and I will know, not the word of those who are puffed up, but the power. For the kingdom of God is not in word but in power [dunamis]" [1 Corinthians 4:19,20, NKJV]. In his second letter to the Corinthians, Paul writes: "For it is the God who commanded the light to shine out of darkness, who has shone in our hearts to give the light of the knowledge of the glory of God in the face of Jesus Christ. But we have this treasure in earthen vessels, that the excellence of the power [*dunamis*] may be of God and not of us" [2 Corinthians 4:6,7, NKJV].

"We have this treasure . . ."! Paul says. But "the excellence of the power" is not some magic formula to be exercised at one's own discretion. The "excellence of the power" is according to God's providence at work in us as we "walk by the spirit." Paul recounts how he "pleaded with the Lord three times that it [a thorn in the flesh—a messenger of Satan] might depart from me. And He [the Lord] said to me, 'My grace is sufficient for you, for My strength [*dunamis*] is made perfect in weakness.' Therefore most gladly I will rather boast in my infirmities, in reproaches, in needs, in persecutions, in distresses, for Christ's sake. For when I am weak, then I am strong" [2 Corinthians 12:8-10, NKJV].

In Paul's letter to the Ephesians, which contains the ultimate Church truth, he declares: "Therefore I also, after I heard of your faith in the Lord Jesus and your love for all the saints, do not cease to give thanks for you, making mention of you in my prayers: that the God of our Lord Jesus Christ, the Father of glory, may give to you the spirit of wisdom and revelation in the knowledge of Him, the eyes of your understanding being enlightened; that you may know what is the hope of His calling, what are the riches of the glory of His inheritance in the saints, and what is the exceeding greatness of His power [*dunamis*] toward us who believe, according to the working of His mighty power [*dunamis*] which He worked in Christ when He raised Him from the dead and seated Him at His right hand in the heavenly places . . ." [Ephesians 1:15-20, NKJV]. As well, Paul prays "that He [God] would grant you, according to the riches of His glory, to be strengthened with might [*dunamis*] through His Spirit in the inner man . . . Now to Him who is able to do exceedingly abundantly above all that we ask or think, according to the power [*dunamis*] that works in us . . ." [Ephesians 3:20, 21, NKJV]. The Scriptures state it clearly: the power works in us!

"Finally, my brethren," Paul says in Ephesians 6, "be strong [*endunamoo*-"endued with strength, be enabled"] in the Lord and in the power [*kratos*-"mighty deed, force"] of His might [*eschus*-"strength, ability"]. Put on the whole armor of God . . ." [Ephesians 6:10,11, NKJV]. We will have more to say about "the whole armor of God" in chapter 6.

Paul's letters to the Thessalonians are thought to be his first epistles to the churches. He says to them, "For our gospel did not come to you in word only, but also in power [*dunamis*], and in the Holy Spirit and in much assurance . . ." [1 Thessalonians 1:5, NKJV]. Later he exhorts the believers: "Therefore we also pray always for you that our God would count you worthy of this calling, and fulfill all the good pleasure of His goodness and the work of faith with power [*dunamis*], that the name of our Lord Jesus Christ may be glorified in you . . ." [2 Thessalonians 1:11,12, NKJV]. In his second letter to his beloved Timothy, he writes: ". . . God has not given us a spirit of fear, but of power [*dunamis*] and of love and of a sound mind" [2Timothy 1:7, NKJV].

Our power of attorney

"And whatever you ask in My name, that I will do, that the Father may be glorified in the Son. If you ask anything in My name, I will do it" [John 13,14, NKJV]. Our Lord Jesus Christ has given each member of His spiritual Body the legal right to use His name for good. When God raised Jesus from the dead and "highly exalted Him," He gave His Son "the name that is above every name, that at the name of Jesus every knee should bow, of those in heaven, and of those on earth, and of those under the earth, and that every tongue should confess that Jesus Christ is Lord, to the glory of God the Father" [Philippians 2:9-11, NKJV]. "And these signs will follow those who believe:" the Lord says in Mark 16. "In My name they will cast out demons; they will speak with new tongues; they will take up serpents; and if they drink anything deadly, it will by no means hurt them; they will lay hands on the sick, and they will recover" [Mark 16:17,18, NKJV]. As well, Paul encourages every believer: "And whatever you do in word or deed, do all in the name of the Lord Jesus, giving thanks to God the Father through Him" [Colossians 3:17, NKJV]. And James assures us: "Is anyone among you sick? Let him call for the elders of the church, and let them pray over him, anointing him with oil in the name of the Lord. And the prayer of faith will save [*sozo*-"rescue, restore, deliver"] the sick, and the Lord will raise him up. And if he has committed sins, he will be forgiven" [James 5:14,15, NKJV].

The illuminating records of the history of the early Christian Church which we read in the Acts of the Apostles and in Paul's letters are clear and dramatic: "God has not given us a spirit of fear, but of power"—*dunamis*—strength, ability, inherent power—the same inherent power at work in the Lord Jesus Christ in His earthly ministry. "Our God is able to do exceedingly abundantly above all that we ask or think *according to the power* [*dunamis*-"strength, ability, inherent power"] *at work in us*" [italics supplied]. This is "the Promise of the Father" prophesied by our Lord, the promised "power from on high," the "Counselor," the "Helper"—"the Spirit of truth" at work in those who believe. Our God is able. But is our God willing?

Summary
"Power from on High"

The "Promise of the Father" is "power from on high" inherent in the baptism in holy spirit which the Lord has poured out on every believer in Him. The Scriptures state it clearly: the power works in us!

Verse to Remember: "Our God is able to do exceedingly abundantly above all that we ask or think according to the power at work in us" [Ephesians 3:20,21, NKJV].

Questions to ask Myself: Have I received into evidence the baptism in holy spirit? Do I have faith that the power works in me?

Exercise: When I awaken in the night hours, I will commune with my Heavenly Father, I will praise Him, I will cast my care upon Him because He cares for me, and I will thank Him for renewed purpose for my life. I will pour out my heart before Him [Psalm 62:8].

THREE

"He healed them all"

"I am the Lord who heals you," God assures His people in Exodus 15. But certain conditions were attached to God's promise of healing: "If you diligently heed the voice of the Lord your God and do what is right in His sight, give ear to His commandments and keep all of His statutes, I will put none of the diseases on you which I have brought on the Egyptians. For I am the Lord who heals you" [v.26, NKJV].

Does God still heal people today? And if so, why is it that some people who come to God to be healed fail to receive healing? The psalmist, considering the children of Israel's transgressions against God's commandments, says: "Fools, because of their transgression, and because of their iniquities, were afflicted. Their soul abhorred all manner of food and they drew near to the gates of death. Then they cried out to the Lord in their trouble, and He saved them out of their distresses. He sent His word and healed them, and delivered them from their destructions. Oh that men would give thanks to the Lord for His goodness, and for His wonderful works to the children of men!" [Psalm 107:17-21, NKJV].

"He sent His word and healed them and delivered them from their destructions." This truth becomes singularly important as we continue to develop the scope of this study. John 1:14 tells us that in the person of Jesus Christ ". . . the Word became flesh and dwelt among us, and we beheld His glory, the glory as of the only begotten of the Father, full of grace and truth" [NKJV]. And verse 18: "No one has seen God at any time, the only begotten Son, who is in the bosom of the Father, He has declared Him." Jesus Christ—"in the bosom [*kolpos*-"the fold, hollow, blessedness"] of the Father," "declared" [*exegeomai*-"unfolded, led out, fully made known"] God's love, mercy, kindness, and purpose in His

15

teaching, by His actions, through the fullness of His ministry. In John 10:30 Jesus says: "I and My Father are one" [NKJV], meaning "one in purpose." One vital aspect of the Lord's "declaring" God's purpose and love for His people was that, at every opportunity, as great multitudes followed Him, He "healed them all" [Matthew 12:15, NKJV.]

Matthew reports in his gospel: "And Jesus went about all Galilee, teaching in their synagogues, preaching the gospel of the kingdom, and healing all kinds of sickness among the people" [Matthew 4:23, NKJV]. ". . . They brought to Him many who were demon possessed. And He cast out the spirits with a word, and healed all who were sick" [8:16]. "Then Jesus went about all the cities and villages, teaching in their synagogues, preaching the gospel of the kingdom, and healing every sickness and every disease among the people" [9:35]. "And when He had called His twelve disciples to Him, He gave them power over unclean spirits, to cast them out, and to heal all kinds of sickness and all kinds of disease" [10:1]. "These twelve Jesus sent out and commanded them: ' . . . heal the sick, cleanse the lepers, raise the dead, cast out demons. Freely you have received, freely give'" [10:5a,8]. "And when Jesus went out He saw a great multitude; and He was moved with compassion for them, and healed their sick" [14:14]. "Then great multitudes came to Him, having with them the lame, blind, mute, maimed, and many others, and they laid them down at Jesus' feet, and He healed them" [15:30]. "And great multitudes followed Him, and He healed them there" [19:2]. "Then the blind and the lame came to Him in the temple, and He healed them" [21:14].

Mark reports in his gospel: "Then He healed many who were sick with various diseases, and cast out many demons; and did not allow the demons to speak, because they knew Him" [1:34, NKJV]. "For He healed many, so that as many as had afflictions pressed about Him to touch Him" [3:10]. "And He called the twelve to Himself and began to send them out two by two, and gave them power over unclean spirits . . . So they went out and preached that people should repent. And they cast out many demons, and anointed with oil many who were sick, and healed them" [6:7,12,13].

Luke reports in his gospel: "When the sun was setting, all those who had any that were sick with various diseases brought them to Him; and He laid His hands on every one of them and healed them" [4:40, NKJV]. "Now it happened on another Sabbath, also, that He entered the synagogue and taught. And a man was there whose right hand was withered . . . He said to the man, 'Stretch out your hand.' And he did so, and his hand was restored as whole as the other" [6:6, 10a]. "And the whole multitude sought to touch Him for power went out from Him and healed them all" [6:19]. "And the twelve were with Him, and certain women who had been healed of evil spirits and infirmities—Mary called Magdalene, out of whom had come seven demons . . ." [8:1b,2]. "Then they went out to see what had happened, and came to Jesus, and found the man from whom the demons had departed, sitting at the feet of Jesus, clothed and in his right mind. And they were afraid" [8:35]. "Then He called His twelve disciples together and gave them power and authority over all demons, and to cure diseases. He sent them to preach the kingdom of God and to heal the sick . . . So they departed and went through the towns, preaching the gospel and healing everywhere . . . And the apostles, when they returned, told Him all that they had done. Then He took them and went aside privately into a deserted place belonging to the city called Bethsaida. But when the multitude knew it, they followed Him; and He received them and spoke to them about the kingdom of God, and healed those who were in need of healing" [9:1,2,6,10,11]. "Suddenly a man from the multitude cried out, saying, 'Teacher, I implore You, look on my son, for he is my only child. And behold, a spirit seizes him, and he suddenly cries out; it convulses him so that he foams at the mouth; and it departs from him with great difficulty, bruising him. So I implored Your disciples to cast it out, but they could not' . . . Then Jesus rebuked the unclean spirit, healed the child, and gave him back to his father. And they were all amazed at the majesty of God" [9:38-40, 42b]. "And behold, there was a certain man before Him who had dropsy. And Jesus, answering, spoke to the lawyers and Pharisees, saying, 'Is it lawful to heal on the Sabbath?' But they kept silent. And He took him and healed him, and let him go" [14:2-4].

"Loose him, and let him go."

John reports in his gospel: "The thief does not come except to steal, and to kill, and to destroy. I have come that they may have life, and that they may have it more abundantly" [John 10:10, NKJV]. "I have come," Jesus says, "that they may have life . . . ." In the Greek text the word for "life" is *zoe* which means "the absolute fullness of life, both essential and ethical." This one verse states the Lord's whole purpose in presenting God to humanity. In John 11 He says to Martha: "I am the resurrection and the life. He who believes in Me, though he may die, he shall live." Then he said, "Did I not say to you that if you would believe you would see the glory of God? . . . Now when He had said these things, He cried with a loud voice, 'Lazarus, come forth!' And he who had died came out bound hand and foot with grave clothes, and his face was wrapped with a cloth. Jesus said to them, 'Loose him, and let him go'" [John 11:25,40,43,44, NKJV]. The raising of Lazarus from the dead was in fulfillment of Jesus' prophecy about Himself from Luke 4: "The Spirit of the Lord is upon Me, Because He has anointed Me to proclaim liberty to the captives . . ." and "To set at liberty those who are oppressed . . . ." "The words that I speak to you," He says in John 14, "I do not speak on My own authority; but the Father who dwells in Me does the works. Believe Me that I am in the Father and the Father in Me, or else believe Me for the sake of the works themselves. Most assuredly, I say to you, he who believes in Me, the works that I do he will do also, and greater works than these he will do, because I go to My Father. And whatever you ask in My name, that will I do, that the Father may be glorified in the Son. If you ask anything in My name, I will do it" [John 14:10b-14, NKJV]. Jesus said that He came that believers in Him might have "life"—*zoe*— "the absolute fullness of life," not only in this present existence but also in that which is to come: "I am the resurrection and the life" [life that is everlasting].

In record after record the Gospels inform us that Jesus Christ was enabled by God with power [*dunamis*-"inherent ability"] and authority [*exousia*-"permission, freedom"] to heal and to "set the captives free," and that He healed the people *at every opportunity.* "I can of Myself do nothing," He said. "As I hear, I judge; and My judgment is righteous, because I do not seek My own will but the will of the Father who sent Me" [John 5:30, NKJV]. Is it the will of our Heavenly Father to heal? Clearly, in the ministry of His Son, God demonstrated His ability and willingness to heal *at every opportunity.* What's more, Jesus promised that this same power and authority would be given to His disciples.

Acts chapter 5 tells of this remarkable fulfillment of the Lord's promise: "And through the hands of the apostles many signs and wonders were done among the people . . . so that they brought the sick out in the streets and laid them on beds and couches, that at least the shadow of Peter passing by might fall on some of them. Also a multitude gathered from surrounding cities to Jerusalem, bringing sick people and those who were tormented by unclean spirits, and they were all healed" [Acts 5:12a, 15, 16, NKJV].

Philip was one of the first deacons in the early Church, not an apostle, yet his ministry on behalf of the Lord was confirmed by signs, miracles, and wonders. "Then Philip went down to the city of Samaria and preached Christ to them. And the multitudes with one accord headed the things spoken by Philip, hearing and seeing the miracles which he did. For unclean spirits, crying with a loud voice, came out of many who were possessed; and many who were paralyzed and lame were healed. And there was great joy in that city" [Acts 8:5-8, NKJV].

The ministry of the apostle Paul was confirmed by signs, miracles, and wonders. "Now it happened in Iconium that they [Paul and Barnabas] went together to the synagogue of the Jews, and so spoke that a great multitude both of the Jews and of the Greeks believed . . . Therefore they stayed there a long time, speaking boldly in the Lord, who was bearing witness to the word of His grace, granting signs and wonders to be done by their hands . . . And in Lystra a certain man without strength in his feet was sitting, a cripple from his mother's womb, who had never walked. This man heard Paul speaking. Paul, observing him intently and seeing that he had faith to be healed, said with a loud voice, 'Stand up straight on your feet!' And he leaped and walked" [Acts 14:1,3,8-10, NKJV].

On Paul's journey to Rome, on the island of Malta, ". . . when Paul had gathered a bundle of sticks and laid them on the fire, a viper came out because of the heat, and fastened on his hand. So when the natives saw the creature hanging from his hand, they said to one another, 'No doubt this man is a murderer, whom, though he has escaped the sea, yet justice does not allow to live.' But he shook off the creature into the fire and suffered no harm. However they were expecting that he would swell up or suddenly fall down dead. But after they had looked for a long time and saw no harm come to him, they changed their minds and said that he was a god. In that region there was an estate of the leading citizen of that island, whose name was Publius, who received us and entertained us courteously for three days. And it happened that the father of Publius lay sick of a fever and dysentery. Paul went in to him and prayed, and he laid his hands on him and healed him. So when this was done, the rest of those on the island who had diseases also came and were healed" [Acts 28:3-9, NKJV].

In his first letter to the Corinthians, Paul writes: ". . . my speech and my preaching were not with persuasive words of human wisdom, but in demonstration of the Spirit and of power, that your faith should not be in the wisdom of men but in the power of God" [1 Corinthians 2:4,5, NKJV]. And in 1 Corinthians 12, he elucidates fully on this "demonstration of the Spirit and of power" in his discourse on the "manifestation of the Spirit" which is "given to each one for the profit of all." This "manifestation of the Spirit" includes "discerning of spirits," "gifts of healings," and "the working of miracles." [More on the manifestations of the spirit in chapter 5.] Paul concludes: "Now you are the body of Christ, and members individually. And God has appointed these in the church: first apostles, second prophets, third teachers, after that miracles, then gifts of healings, helps, administrations, varieties of tongues" [1 Corinthians 12:7, 27,28, NKJV]. God has *appointed* miracles and gifts of healings in the Church.

The evidence in God's word is overwhelmingly conclusive: "I am the Lord who heals you." "Therefore," Paul says in Hebrews 12, "strengthen the hands which hang down, and the feeble knees and make straight paths for your feet, so that what is lame may not be dislocated, but rather be healed" [vss. 12,13, NKJV].

James, the Lord's brother, says: "Confess your trespasses to one another, and pray for one another, that you may be healed. The effective, fervent prayer of a righteous man avails much" [James 5:16, NKJV].

The prophet Isaiah, looking forward 700 years by revelation from God to the passion of the Messiah, said: "Surely He has born our griefs and carried our sorrows; yet we esteemed Him stricken, smitten by God and afflicted. But He was wounded for our transgressions, He was bruised for our iniquities; the chastisement for our peace was upon Him, and by His stripes we are healed" [Isaiah 53:4,5, NKJV].

The apostle Peter, looking back on the Lord's ministry and his own personal experience at the Lord's side, writes: ". . . who Himself bore our sins in His own body on the tree, that we, having died to sin, might live for righteousness—by whose stripes you were healed" [1 Peter 2:24, NKJV]. Gifts of healings are *appointed* by God in the Church because His Son suffered stripes on our behalf.

The apostle John concludes: "Beloved, I pray that you may prosper in all things and be in health, just as your soul prospers" [3 John 2, NKJV]. It is our Heavenly Father's desire that every one of His children prosper and be in health.

"God is love."

The essential nature, character, and purpose of God, revealed to us in the Holy Scriptures, assures us that God's intense desire is to heal His people. 1 John 4:16 says that "God is love." Love is God's very nature—His unchanging character. Moreover, He is "the Father of mercies and the God of all comfort" [2 Corinthians 1:3, NKJV]. Some may ask: "What about Romans 8:28 which reads: 'And we know that all things work together for good to those who love God . . . '"[NKJV], interpreting this verse to mean that all things—even bad things—are ultimately the will of God for those who love Him. The NIV translates this verse: "And we know that in all things God works for the good of those who love him . . . ." *In all things* God works for our good according to our believing faith. This is not to say that all things are good or that all things are God's will. Some things are the result of accidents and bad luck due to the nature of life in this fallen world (Ecclesiastes 9:11b: "But time and chance happen to them all."); and some things come from the god of this world which 1 John 5:18 labels "the wicked one."

In Genesis 1:31 we see God's original plan and purpose for mankind: "Then God saw everything that He had made, and indeed it was very good" [NKJV]. God's original plan and purpose for people was *paradise on earth,* free from sickness, disease, and death, plus everlasting fellowship with Him. As the result of their disobedience, Adam and Eve ushered in sin and corruption. God's original plan and purpose for His people will ultimately be fulfilled in *paradise restored* to the earth, as described in John's Revelation of Jesus Christ.

"fearfully and wonderfully made"

David declares in Psalm 139:14: "I will praise you, for I am fearfully and wonderfully made" [NKJV]. Some people believe that God puts sickness and disease on people in order to test their faith. Physicians know that the human body is designed to heal itself if given a chance. If God puts sickness and disease on people, then God would be working *against* Himself—against His very nature which is love, against the divine design of the human body to heal itself, against His expressed purpose and plan in the life, teaching, ministry of deliverance and ultimate sacrifice of His only begotten Son, Jesus Christ.

If God's desire for His people is that they be healed, then why is it that many who come to God seeking healing are not healed? There are reasons. "I am the Lord who heals you," God told the children of Israel. At the same time He warned them: "If you diligently heed the voice of the Lord your God and do what is right in His sight, give ear to His commandments and keep all of His statutes, I will put none of the diseases on you which I have put on the Egyptians." This promise was given specifically to the children of Israel who were subject to the Law of Moses. Believers today are not under the Law. Romans 10:4 says, "For Christ is the end of the law for righteousness to everyone who believes" [NKJV]. However, few Christians understand this truth, let alone believe it. Most Christians in our times are what Paul calls "carnal"—that is, living according to the desires of the flesh rather than walking by the spirit of God born in them. "I fed you with milk and not with solid food," Paul writes to the Corinthians, "for until now you were not able to receive it, and even now you are still not able; for you are still carnal" [1 Corinthians 2,3a, NKJV]. And he says to the Galatians: "I say then: Walk in the Spirit, and you shall not fulfill the lust of the flesh. For the flesh lusts against the Spirit and the Spirit against the flesh; and these are contrary to one another, so that you do not do the things that you wish" [Galatians 5:16,17, NKJV]. Paul says to the Romans: ". . . do not let sin reign in your mortal body, that you should obey it in its lusts" [Romans 6:12, NKJV]. Sin—which is separation from God—defeats the promises of God in the lives of many Christians so that they do not "diligently heed the voice of the Lord" and "give ear to His commandments." James says: ". . . be doers of the word, and not hearers only, deceiving yourselves" [James 1:22, NKJV]. Again: "If any of you lacks wisdom, let him ask of God, who gives to all liberally and without reproach, and it will be given to him. But let him ask in faith, with no doubting, for he who doubts is like a wave of the sea driven and tossed by the wind. For let not that man suppose that he will receive anything from the Lord; he is a double-minded man, unstable in all his ways" [James 1:5-8, NKJV].

Regarding faith—or lack of it—Matthew tells us that when "Jesus had come to His own country, he taught them in their synagogue, so that they were astonished and said, 'Where did this man get this wisdom and these mighty works? Is this not the carpenter's son? Is not His mother called Mary? And his brothers James, Joses, Simon, and Judas? And His sisters, are they not all with us? When then did this man get all these things?' So they were offended at Him. But Jesus said to them, 'A prophet is not without honor except in his own country and in his own house.' Now He did not do many mighty works there because of their unbelief" [Matthew 13:54-58, NKJV]. Unbelief defeats the promises of God! Lack of faith in God's willingness to heal and in the spiritual power and authority of the person ministering healing defeats many Christians today. Few are taught the truth about every believer's spiritual standing in Christ. Most churches promote adherence to the Ten Commandments and other dictates of the Law instead of this "grace in which we stand" [Romans 5:2] and the astounding truth that the risen and glorified Christ has become for us "wisdom from God—and righteousness and sanctification and redemption . . ." [1 Corinthians 1:30, NKJV]. As well, in a fervid quest for healing, many Christians are held spellbound by the charismatic personality of certain teachers they perceive as having a "special anointing" so that their faith is in the teacher and not in the power and authority of the gift of holy spirit born in every person who comes to Christ. The truth is, this "anointing" is in *you*.

Summary
"He healed them all"

The evidence in God's word is overwhelming: "I am the Lord who heals you."

Verse to Remember: "The thief does not come except to steal, and to kill, and to destroy. I have come that they may have life, and that they may have it more abundantly" [John 10:10, NKJV].

Question to ask Myself: Do I believe that God heals people today as He did in the past, according to the Scriptures?

Exercise: Do I have a strong desire to be a prayer intercessor for my family and friends? What are my spiritual strengths, my special skills for service, my gifts from the Lord? I will talk to the Lord about this, and I will pray more than I've ever prayed before. I will converse with the Lord often—because He is my best friend.

FOUR

"The anointing"

At the onset of His ministry following His baptism in holy spirit and testing for forty days in the wilderness, Jesus returns to Nazareth, enters the synagogue, takes the scroll of the prophet Isaiah and reads: "The Spirit of the Lord is upon Me, because He has anointed Me to preach the gospel to the poor . . ." [Luke 4:18a, NKJV]. In the Greek text the word for "anointed" is *chrio* from which also comes the word *chrisma*. *Chrio* means "to rub, to besmear;" *chrisma* is translated "anointing" or "unction." In Acts 4 Peter confirms the Lord's "anointing:" "For truly against Your holy Servant Jesus, whom You anointed [*chrio*], both Herod and Pontius Pilate, with the Gentiles and the people of Israel, were gathered together to do whatever Your hand determined before to be done" [vss. 27,28, NKJV]. And in Acts 10:38 he explains to the household of Cornelius ". . . how God anointed [*chrio*] Jesus of Nazareth with the Holy Spirit and with power, who went about doing good and healing all who were oppressed by the devil, for God was with Him."

Significantly, Peter declares to the Corinthians: "Now He who establishes us with you in Christ and has anointed [*chrio*] us is God" [2 Corinthians 1:21, NKJV]. Thus Paul claims a like anointing that was upon Jesus for his own ministry. Also significantly, in his first epistle, John says: "But you [believers] have an anointing [*chrio*] from the Holy One, and you know all things" [1 John 2:20, NKJV]. Then in verse 27 he says: "But the anointing [*chrisma*] which you have received [*lambano*-"received into evidence"] from Him abides in you . . . ." The "anointing"—the spiritual "rubbing in" which every believer has received from the Lord—"abides" [*meno*—"remains, continues"] in us—it dwells and remains in us. An anointing like Jesus received from His Heavenly Father, which Peter received, which Paul received, which

John received, abides in us! We have this anointing! The problem is, few Christians believe it.

Jesus promised His disciples: "For John truly baptized with water, but you shall be baptized with the Holy Spirit . . . ,""and "you shall receive [*lambano*-"take up, receive into evidence"] power [*dunamis*-"strength, ability"] when the Holy Spirit has come upon you . . ." [Acts 1:5,8, NKJV]. To be "baptized" [*baptizo*] in holy spirit means "to immerse, submerge, consecrate" in the sense of a "pouring out on" or "putting into." Jesus promised His disciples that when they would be baptized in holy spirit, it would be a spiritual "pouring into"—a complete immersion in *dunamis*—power, strength, and authority—to be witnesses unto Him to "the end of the earth." This spiritual "pouring into" was to be like the power and authority He exercised in His earthly ministry, for "he who believes in Me, the works that I do shall He do also, and greater works than these shall he do . . . ."

The baptism in holy spirit, beginning on the Day of Pentecost, was "the Promise of the Father"—the "power from on high"—the "Spirit of truth"—the "Counselor," "Comforter," "Helper"—that Jesus Christ promised to all who would believe in Him immediately and ultimately: "If anyone loves Me, he will keep My word; and My Father will love him, and We will come to him and make Our home with him . . . These things I have spoken to you while being present with you. But the Helper, the Holy Spirit, whom My Father will send in My name, He will teach you all things, and bring to your remembrance all things that I said to you" [John 14:23,25, NKJV].

"If anyone thirsts . . ."

"On the last day, that great day of the feast, Jesus stood and cried out, saying, 'If anyone thirsts, let him come to Me and drink. He who believes in Me, as the Scripture has said, out of his heart will flow rivers of living water.' But this He spoke concerning the Spirit, whom those believing in Him would receive [*lambano*-"receive into evidence"]; for the Holy Spirit was not yet given, because Jesus was not yet glorified" [John 7:37-39, NKJV].

Many have wondered, "How does one receive the baptism in holy spirit?" In John 16 Jesus says: "Most assuredly, I say to you, whatever you ask the Father in My name He will give you. Until now you have asked nothing in My name. Ask, and you will receive, that your joy may be full" [vss. 23,24, NKJV]. And in Luke 11: "So I say to you, ask, and it will be given to you; seek, and you will find; knock, and it will be opened to you. For everyone who asks receives [*lambano*-"receives into evidence"], and he who seeks finds, and to him who knocks it will be opened. If a son asks for bread from any father among you, will he give him a stone? Or if he asks for a fish, will he give him a serpent instead of a fish? Or if he asks for an egg, will he offer him a scorpion? If you then, being evil, know how to give good gifts to your children, how much more will your heavenly Father give the Holy Spirit to those who ask Him?" [vss. 9-13, NKJV].

Jesus promised: ". . . We will come to him and make Our home with him . . . ," and ". . . out of his heart will flow rivers of living water." This "spirit of truth" was at work in Paul when he was inspired to write to the Colossians regarding "the mystery which has been hidden from ages and from generations, but now has been revealed to His saints. To them God willed to make known what are the riches of the glory of this mystery among the Gentiles which is Christ in you, the hope of glory" [Colossians 1:26,27, NKJV]. To have "Christ in you" *is* to be anointed by God.

"Christ in you"

"Christ in you" is the spiritual enablement to be like Christ by means of the baptism in holy spirit. Indeed, the spirit of "Christ in you" is "the *riches* of the glory of this mystery . . . ." In 2 Corinthians 5:17, we learn that ". . . if anyone is in Christ, he is a new creation . . . ." The Greek words are *kainos ktisis. Kainos* means "recently made, fresh, new kind, unprecedented, unheard of." *Ktisis* means "a founding, establishment, thing created." The "new creation" of "Christ in you" is something that is *brand new*, something that did not exist prior to Pentecost. The "new creation" in Christ is very different from what God gave to believers in Old Testament times. It became available only after Christ was raised from the dead and ascended to the Father, that is, after He was glorified. This "new creation" is the unprecedented spiritual enablement not only to walk in the same potential effectiveness as Jesus walked but also to be "transformed into the same image [of the glorified Christ] from glory to glory, just as by the Spirit of the Lord" [2

Corinthians 3:18, NKJV]. The NIV states this more clearly: "And we all, who with unveiled faces contemplate the Lord's glory, are being transformed into his image with ever-increasing glory, which comes from the Lord, who is the Spirit." The point is, it's not our physical bodies that are presently being transformed as we "walk in the light"—it's our *character.* Furthermore, 1 John 3:2 says: "Dear friends, now we are children of God, and what we will be has not yet been made known. But we know that when Christ appears, we shall be like him, for we shall see him as he is" [NKJV]. And Paul says: "For now we see in a mirror, dimly, but then face to face. Now I know in part, but then I shall know just as also I am known" [1 Corinthians 13:12, NKJV]. In our present mortal lives, faithful believers are being transformed in *character.* When we see Him "face to face," our bodies will be transformed into His likeness: "For our citizenship is in heaven, from which we also eagerly wait for the Savior, the Lord Jesus Christ, who will transform our lowly body that it may be conformed to His glorious body, according to the working by which He is able even to subdue all things to Himself" [Philippians 3:20,21, NKJV]. Thus the *process* of our spiritual transformation will be completed at the Rapture [Latin: *rapere;* Greek: *harpazo-*"caught up, seized, snatched away" [1 Thessalonians 4:16-18] of the Church, for "we shall see Him as He is."

"sealed with the Holy Spirit of promise"

Paul provides further insight into this promise of God when he says to the Ephesians: "In Him [Christ] also we have obtained an inheritance, being predestined according to the purpose of Him [God] who works all things according to the counsel of His will, that we who first trusted in Christ should be to the praise of His glory. In Him you also trusted, after you heard the word of truth, the gospel of your salvation; in whom also having believed, you were sealed with the Holy Spirit of promise, who is the guarantee of our inheritance until the redemption of the purchased possession, to the praise of His glory" [Ephesians 1:11-14, NKJV]. And in Ephesians 4 he says: "And do not grieve the Holy Spirit of God by whom you were sealed for the day of redemption" [v.30, NKJV]. Paul assures us that "having believed the word of truth . . . (we) were sealed [*sphragio-*"marked, confirmed, authenticated"] with the Holy Spirit of promise." This "seal" of holy spirit is permanent in the believer in Christ. It cannot be lost. Believers are "sealed" for the day of redemption which is the "Rapture" or "gathering together" of the Church "to meet the Lord in the air" [1 Thessalonians 4:17, NKJV]. Paul explains further in Romans 8: "For as many who are led by the Spirit of God, these are the sons of God. For you did not receive [*lambano*-"receive into evidence"] the spirit of bondage again to fear, but you have received [*lambano*] the spirit of adoption by whom we cry out 'Abba, Father.' The Spirit Himself bears witness with our spirit that we are the children of God, and if children, then heirs—heirs of God and joint heirs with Christ . . ." [8:14-17a, NKJV]. And in his second letter to Timothy: "Therefore I remind you to stir up the gift of God which is in you through the laying on of my hands. For God has not given us a spirit of fear, but of power [*dunamis*] and of love and of a sound mind" [2 Timothy 1:6,7, NKJV].

Peter provides more insight regarding the baptism in holy spirit: "Since you [believers] have purified your souls in obeying the truth through the Spirit in sincere love of the brethren, love one another fervently with a pure heart, having been born again [*anagennao*-"begotten anew"] not of corruptible seed [mortal], but incorruptible [spiritual] through the word of God which lives and abides forever" [1 Peter 1:23, NKJV]. For the believer in Christ, to be "born again" is to be "sealed with the Holy Spirit of promise." In John 3 Jesus tells Nicodemus: "Most assuredly I say to you, unless one is born again [*gennao anothen*-"fathered from heaven, begotten from above"] he cannot see the kingdom of God" [John 3:3, NKJV]. In this context Jesus is talking to a leader of the Jews, a member of the Sanhedrin Council, whom he says in verse 10 ought to have known that He was speaking about the kingdom of God promised at the "resurrection of life" [John 5:29]. Jesus was not speaking about Christians needing to be "born again," but rather in regard to the future promise of God to Israel. However, the concept of "begotten from above" is the same for both future Israel and the Christian Church: Regarding the "resurrection of life," Jesus says: ". . . that which is born of the flesh is flesh, and that which is born of the Spirit is Spirit. Do not marvel that I said to you, you must be born again" [John 3:6,7, NKJV]. Regarding the Rapture of the Christian Church, Paul writes: "Now this I say, brethren, that flesh and blood cannot inherit the kingdom of God; nor does corruption inherit incorruption. Behold, I tell you a mystery: We shall not all sleep, but we shall all be changed—in a moment, in the twinkling of an eye, at the last trumpet. For the trumpet will sound, and the dead will be raised incorruptible, and we shall be changed. For this corruptible must put on incorruption, and this mortal must put on immortality" [1 Corinthians 15:51-53, NKJV].

John 4:24 tells us that "God is Spirit . . . ." Therefore the spiritual "seed" of God is holy spirit, and whoever is "born" of God —"born again, born from above"— receives the "incorruptible" seed which is the everlasting spirit of God. In 1 John 5: "Whoever believes that Jesus is the Christ is born [gennao-"fathered, begotten"] of God, and everyone who loves Him who begot also loves him who is begotten of Him . . . For whatever is born of God overcomes the world [kosmos-"world system, arrangement"]. And this is the victory that has overcome the world [system]—our faith" [v. 1,4, NKJV]. It is the Christian's "faith"—believing faith that he is "born from above," "born of incorruptible seed," baptized in holy spirit, immersed and clothed in "power from on high," that can, in its day-by-day potential, help him to overcome the world system. This is the "Promise of the Father" and the assurance of the active ministry of "Christ in you, the hope of glory." Thus Paul is not boasting when he declares: "I can do all things through Christ who strengthens me" [endynamoo-"endues, increases in strength"] [Philippians 4:13, NKJV]. Indeed, Paul's ministry as an apostle was characterized and authenticated by the signs, miracles, and wonders which he accomplished by means of the spirit [the pneuma, the dunamis] of Christ in him. Paul says to the Thessalonians: "For our gospel did not come to you in word only, but also in power [dunamis], and in the Holy Spirit, and in much assurance, as you know what kind of men we were among you for your sake" [1 Thessalonians 1:5, NKJV]. Then he says, "Rejoice always, pray without ceasing, in everything give thanks; for this is the will of God in Christ Jesus for you. Do not quench [sbennumi-"extinguish, stifle, suppress"] the Spirit. Do not despise prophesies. Test all things; hold fast that what is good" [5:16-21, NKJV]. "Therefore," he says, "we also pray always for you that our God would count you worthy of this calling, and fulfill all the good pleasure of His goodness and the work of faith with power [dunamis], that the name of our Lord Jesus Christ may be glorified in you" [2 Thessalonians 1:11,12a, NKJV]. As well, Acts 19 informs us that "God worked unusual miracles by the hands of Paul, so that even handkerchiefs or aprons were brought from his body to the sick, and the diseases left them and the evil spirits went out of them" [Acts 19:11,12, NKJV].

To the Corinthians Paul says: "Now He who establishes us with you in Christ and has anointed us is God, who also has sealed us and given us the Spirit in our hearts as a guarantee" [2 Corinthians 1:21,22, NKJV]. To the Galatians he says: "Christ has redeemed us from the curse of the law, having become a curse for us (for it is written, 'Cursed is everyone who hangs on a tree,' that the blessing of Abraham might come upon the Gentiles in Christ Jesus, that we might receive [*lambano*-"receive into evidence"] the promise of the Spirit through faith" [Galatians 3:13,14, NKJV]. And: "I say then, walk in the Spirit and you shall not fulfill the lust of the flesh. For the flesh lusts against the Spirit, and the Spirit against the flesh; and these are contrary to one another, so that you do not do the things that you wish. But if you are led by the Spirit, you are not under the law . . . But the fruit [*karpos*-"effect, result, profit"] of the Spirit is love, joy, peace, longsuffering, kindness, goodness, faithfulness, gentleness, self-control. Against such there is no law" [Galatians 5:16-18,22, NKJV].

"a dwelling place of God"

And to the Ephesians Paul says: "Now, therefore, you are no longer strangers and foreigners, but fellow citizens with the saints and members of the household of God, having been built on the foundation of the apostles and prophets, Jesus Christ Himself being the chief cornerstone, in whom the whole building, being fitted together, grows into a holy temple in the Lord, in whom you also are being built together for a dwelling place of God in the Spirit" [Ephesians 2:19-22, NKJV]. And also: "For this reason I bow my knees to the Father of our Lord Jesus Christ, from whom the whole family in heaven and earth is named, that He would grant you, according to the riches of His glory, to be strengthened [*krataioo*-"to grow strong"] with might [*dunamis*] through His Spirit in the inner man [the "Christ in you"] . . . Now to Him who is able to do exceedingly abundantly above all that we ask or thing according to the power [*dunamis*] that works in us, to Him be glory in the church by Christ Jesus forever and ever. Amen" [Ephesians 3:14-16, 20, 21, NKJV].

Glory in the Church—the body of Christ! There can be glory in the Church only when God's people rise up in believing faith to "walk by the spirit" and operate d*unamis*—the inherent spiritual strength that the Lord has given us—and exercise e*xousia*—the authority to use the name of Jesus Christ for good. For every believer in Christ is anointed with "Christ in you!"

"Therefore," Paul says to the Ephesians, "take up the whole armor of God, that you may be able to withstand in the evil day, and having done all, to stand . . . and take the helmet of salvation, and the sword of the Spirit, which is the world of God; praying always with all prayer and supplication in the Spirit" [Ephesians 6:13, 17, 18, NKJV]. [Chapter 6 provides more insight into the "whole armor of God."]

Summary
"The anointing"

To be baptized in holy spirit is to have "Christ in you," which is to be anointed by God.

Verse to Remember: "But the anointing which you have received from Him abides in you" [1 John 2:27, NKJV].

Question to ask Myself: Do I believe I have God's anointing on my life, or do I feel that is only for others more worthy than I?

Exercise: This is my confession: "I am a new creation in Christ! I am clothed with "power from on high." I am "born from above"— "sealed with the Holy Spirit of promise." "I am anointed by God!" "Seeing then that we have a great High Priest who has passed through the heavens, Jesus the Son of God, let us hold fast our confession" [Hebrews 4:14, NKJV].

FIVE

"Now concerning *pneumatikos*"

"**N**ow concerning spiritual *gifts*, brethren, I do not want you to be ignorant," Paul writes to the Corinthians [1 Corinthians 12:1, NKJV]. In the Greek text the single word for "spiritual *gifts*" is *pneumatikos*, which means "belonging to the Divine Spirit" or simply "things or matters of the spirit." Alas, in most versions of the Bible, *pneumatikos* is inappropriately translated "spiritual gifts," even though in the NKJV "*gifts*" is in italics, letting the reader know that the word is not in the Greek text. Young's Literal Translation reads: "And concerning the spiritual things . . ." The Darby Translation reads: "But concerning spiritual [manifestations] . . . ." The Douay-Rheims 1899 American Edition reads: "Now concerning spiritual things . . . ." And the Wycliffe New Testament reads: "But of spiritual things . . . ."

Much confusion has persisted in the Church because of the inappropriate translation of *pneumatikos* in the first verse of chapter 12. Likewise, in verse 1 of chapter 14, the NKJV reads: "Pursue love, and desire spiritual *gifts* . . . ." And 1 Corinthians 13:2 reads: "And though I have *the gift of* prophecy . . . ." The words in italics are not in the Greek text. They were added to the English by the translators, thinking that they were clarifying the text. Alas, they merely added confusion. Indeed, when Paul talks about the "manifestations of the Spirit" in verses 7-10, most readers assume that the nine "manifestations" listed are actually individual "gifts" bestowed at God's prerogative. Therefore most students of the Bible believe that surely one can receive no more than two, or at most, three of God's "gifts," such as "tongues" or "the gift of prophecy." Thus it is assumed that only certain "gifted" people—charismatic preachers or "faith healers"—can operate the "gifts" of miracles and healings. But this is not what God's Word teaches in its accuracy.

In 1 Corinthians 12:7 Paul says: "But the manifestation [*phanerosis*-"evidence, unveiling"] of the Spirit is given to each one for the profit of all" [NKJV]. The nine manifestations or evidences of the gift of holy spirit listed in verses 8-10 are not individual gifts given by God to select believers. Rather, they are all evidences of the one gift of holy spirit every born-again believer possesses, and they are all available to be manifested in a believer's life if he or she will learn how to develop and operate them appropriately. Indeed, it is clear in 1 Corinthians 12:7 that a change in subject occurs from that which preceded these verses. In verses 4-6 Paul is talking about "diversities of gifts," "differences of ministries," and "diversities of activities." Verse 7 begins with the word "But." This is the word *de in* the Greek text, which is also translated "now" in other parts of the New Testament. "But" or "Now" indicates a change in subject from the previous discussion. Here Paul begins to talk about something that is given to "each one for the profit of all"—the manifestation of the spirit. Each believer has *dunamis*—"inherent power" and ability potentially to bring into evidence each of the manifestations of the spirit in appropriate circumstances. We might think of the gift of holy spirit like a Swiss army knife. The owner has the potential to use a blade, a screwdriver, a bottle opener, etc., depending on the need. Likewise, with the gift of holy spirit, each believer has the potential to operate any one or several of the manifestations of the spirit for different purposes. Our Heavenly Father has given each of His children the gift of holy spirit to empower and enable us to "walk by the spirit" in the steps of Jesus Christ and thus do the work He wants us to do. Of course, people can be born of holy spirit with all the potential it provides and yet not walk in the power available. Paul says to the Thessalonians: "Do not quench [*sbennumi*-"stifle, suppress"] the Spirit" [1 Thessalonians 5:19, NKJV]. A believer can "quench" the spirit by failing to speak in tongues, or despising prophecies, or failing to "walk by faith, not by sight." Paul calls a believer who lives by his senses only and fails to walk by the spirit a "carnal" Christian. Many believers are in this category, either because they have not been taught how to walk by the spirit or have simply not believed what they've been taught. Our Heavenly Father challenges each of His children not to be conformed to this world but to be "transformed [*metamorphoo*-"changed into another form, transfigured"] by "the renewing of your mind . . ." [Romans 12:2, NKJV], and to "be diligent to present yourselves approved to God, a

worker who does not need to be ashamed . . ." [2 Timothy 2:15,NKJV]. God
wants His children to "grow up" spiritually so they can do the works
that Jesus did and set the captives free, thereby bringing glory to God.
There is only so much that we can accomplish by our own human
ability no matter how educated or talented we may be. In order to truly
help someone, we must operate *dunamis*. The message of 1 Corinthians
12-14 is that each believer ought to speak in tongues much in order
to "edify" his spirit ["He who speaks in a tongue edifies himself"] [1
Corinthians 14:4, NKJV], "desire earnestly to prophesy" in a fellowship for
the edifying of the believers [v. 5], and learn to hear "the still, small of
God" [1 Kings 19:12, NKJV] by means of the manifestations of word of
knowledge, word of wisdom, and discerning of spirits so as to know
what to do in any challenging situation. Every faithful minister of God
who believes in the power of God at work in his ministry knows that
at various times and for different purposes he has received revelation
knowledge and wisdom from the Lord, and that he has been inspired to
bring forth words of prophecy for the building up of his congregation
of believers. Some have even believed to operate the manifestations of
believing faith, miracles, and gifts of healings in order to set the captives
free. Living life "more abundantly," as Jesus promised in John 10:10,
requires spiritual power and authority, and God says this is resident in
every believer via the gift of holy spirit.

That each believer has the potential to operate all nine manifestations
of the spirit is clearly implied in the Greek text of 1 Corinthians 12:7
and 8—however muddied the English translations seem. Moreover,
verse 11 concludes: ". . . one and the same Spirit" [Christ in you!]
works all these things, distributing to each one individually as He wills."
Every believer has the potential to operate any of the manifestations,
but it is the Lord, via the gift of holy spirit, who does the distributing
according to His own purposes and according to the dynamics of the
circumstances. In a fellowship of believers, one may be inspired by the
Lord to speak in tongues out loud and then give the interpretation
in the language of the people present, while another may be inspired
to bring forth a word of prophecy. In a laying-on-of hands service, a
spiritually mature believer praying over and ministering to another,
has available to him all nine manifestations of the spirit. Depending
on his knowledge and understanding of their operation, however,
he may simply pray or prophesy or he may receive revelation word

of knowledge and word of wisdom from the Lord for the operation of discerning of spirits, the working of a miracle or a gift of healing according to his believing faith to obey the Lord's instructions. Many examples of the manifestations of the spirit in operation both in Jesus and in His disciples are presented in chapters 10 and 11. Paul says in any church service, "God is not the author of confusion but of peace, as in all the churches of the saints," and "Let all things be done decently and in order" [1 Corinthians 14:33,40, NKJV].

Much of the heart of God's word and the Lord's specific instructions to the members of His Body are understood fully only when acted upon and lived out. God designed His word to be understood only by faithful disciples—disciplined ones. "If anyone wills to do His [God's] will," Jesus said, "he shall know concerning the doctrine, whether it is from God or whether I speak on My own authority" [John 7:17, NKJV]. It is understood that only people who are faithful in prayer can truly understand the heart and power of prayer. Likewise, only those who earnestly desire the fullness of the spirit at work in their lives can truly understand the operation of the manifestations of the spirit.

The Lord declares emphatically that He does not want His people to be ignorant concerning *pneumatikos*—the things of the spirit. Thus He provides detailed information in 1 Corinthians 12-14 regarding "diversities of gifts," "differences of ministries," and "diversities of activities," but that "the manifestation of the spirit is given to each one for the profit of all."

"speaking in tongues"

The one manifestation of the sprit Paul discusses in these chapters *essential* to the effectual operation of the other manifestations is speaking in tongues. Paul says: "I wish you all spoke with tongues . . ." [1 Corinthians 14:5, NKJV]. "He who speaks in a tongue edifies [*oikodomeo*-"builds up, establishes, strengthens"] himself . . ." [v. 4]. As well, Jude 20 says: "But you, beloved, building yourselves up on your most holy faith, praying in the Holy Spirit, keep yourselves in the love of God . . ."[NKJV]. To pray "in the Holy Spirit" is to speak in tongues. The point Paul makes to the Corinthians is clear: speaking in tongues builds up—spiritually strengthens, edifies— the one speaking, and Paul says it is important that every member of the Body of Christ speaks in tongues. Paul declares this to believers by revelation from the Lord, and it is important to understand that he never would have said it if the spirit in each believer did not *need* edifying. When a person is baptized in the spirit, the gift is perfect in its essence, but it must be edified day by day to enable the believer to "walk by the spirit." In Psalm 46:10 God says "Be still and know that I am God." In I Kings 19:12, God teaches Elijah more perfectly how He communicates by means of the spirit: "'Go out, and stand on the mountain before the Lord.' And behold, the Lord passed by, and a great and strong wind tore into the mountains and broke the rocks and pieces before the Lord, but the Lord was not in the wind; and after the wind an earthquake, but the Lord was not in the earthquake; and after the earthquake a fire, but the Lord was not in the fire; and after the fire a still small voice" [NKJV]. Most of the time God communicates with His children in "a still small voice." Living in this world, we are mentally bombarded daily with the "noise" of the world. In order to "walk by the spirit" and to hear the "still small voice" of God speaking to us by means of the gift of holy spirit—that is, a "word of knowledge" or a "word of wisdom" or the "discerning of spirits," we must edify our spirit every day in order to stay "tuned in" to the spirit and not be overwhelmed by the cacophony of the world around us. Studying the Bible edifies our mind. Speaking in tongues edifies our spirit. Both activities are essential for our walk "in the power of the spirit" as Jesus walked. Therefore Paul says "I would like every one of you to speak in tongues" [NIV], or "I wish you all spoke with tongues" [NKJV]. In this verse in the Greek text the word for "would like" or "wish" is *thelo*, which can be translated "want," as it is in 1 Corinthians 12:1: "Now concerning *pneumatikos,* I do not want [*thelo*] you to be ignorant . . . ." God does not merely *wish* that His people spoke in tongues, He *wants* them to. It is His desire that we all speak in tongues much because He knows the wonderful benefits that speaking in tongues brings to His children. Of course, each one of us has free will, and some will choose to speak in tongues when we understand its value to us and that it is available to do so, and some will choose not to do so either because of misunderstanding or unbelief—or even fear that we are not worthy. Nevertheless, God has made all nine of the manifestations of the spirit available to His children, not because we are worthy in our human selves, but because we need to in order to grow up into Christ who is the head of the Body.

To be clear, speaking in tongues is not an individual gift of God given to those He selects. It is a manifestation of the spirit available to every believer in Christ. Some people first manifest tongues spontaneously upon hearing God's word taught—such as those of the household of Cornelius recorded in Acts 10. Most others, however—because of misunderstanding or wrong teaching or fear—must be taught about the wonderful benefits and privileges of speaking in tongues and then be guided into manifesting. Jesus prophesied: "On the last day of the feast, the great day, Jesus stood up and cried out, 'If anyone thirsts let him come to me and drink. Whoever believes in me, as the Scripture has said, 'Out of his heart [koilia—"innermost being"] will flow rivers of living water.' Now this he said about the Spirit, whom those who believed in him were to receive, for as yet the Spirit had not been given, because Jesus was not yet glorified" [John 7:37-39, ESV]. And in Mark 16:17, He prophesies: "And these signs will accompany those who believe in my name: they will cast out demons; they will speak in new tongues" [ESV]. Those who thirst for all that God has to offer will want to speak in tongues. The truth is, Jesus said we *could,* and Paul said we *should.* Who are we to say we can't?

The benefits of speaking in tongues are wonderful. First, speaking in tongues is perfect praise for our Heavenly Father. The psalmist says: "Yet you are holy, enthroned on the praises of Israel" [Psalm 22:3, ESV]. The ASV reads: "O thou that inhabitest the praises of Israel." God inhabits—is enthroned on—the praises of His people. The people of Israel did not speak in tongues because it was not available until the Day of Pentecost—but whether believers "pray with the spirit"[in tongues] or "pray with the understanding" [in a known language] [1 Corinthians 14:15, NKJV], God "inhabits" the praises of His people. Acts 2:11 informs us that speaking in tongues is speaking "the wonderful works of God." Acts 10:46 says that when those of the household of Cornelius were baptized in holy spirit, Peter and those accompanying him heard them "speak with tongues and magnify God." 1 Corinthians 14:2 says: "For one who speaks in a tongue speaks not to men but to God; for no one understands him; but he utters mysteries in the Spirit" [ESV]. Manifesting the spirit by speaking in tongues "helps in our weakness. For we do not know what to pray for as we ought, but the Spirit himself intercedes for us with groanings too deep for words" [Romans 8:26, ESV]. Romans 8:16 says that "the Spirit himself bears witness with our spirit that we are children of God, and if children, then heirs—heirs of God and fellow heirs with Christ" [ESV].

Speaking in tongues is a God-given language that is either a dialect of mankind or of angels: Paul says, "Though I speak with the tongues of men and of angels . . ." [1 Corinthians 13:1, NKJV]. When a believer speaks in tongues, he does not know the language being spoken. The scripture says that the person does the speaking but the spirit gives the words: "For if I pray in a tongue, my spirit prays, but my understanding is unfruitful" [1 Corinthians 14:14, NKJV].

Speaking in tongues has three basic practical purposes: 1) Perfect praise to God—speaking "the wonderful works of God." 2) The guarantee that the believer is "born from above"—"heir of God and fellow heir with Christ." 3) Edification of the gift of holy spirit. Paul says to the Corinthians: "I thank my God I speak with tongues more than you all" [v.4]. Paul was not boasting; he was making an important point—teaching us that speaking in tongues *much* is necessary for the edification of the spirit.

Some believers fail to speak in tongues even though they've been taught that it is God's will and that it is available to them. They may desire to speak in tongues, but they expect God to take control of their tongues and cause them to speak. God will not do so. Our Heavenly Father has given each of us free will to worship and serve Him or choose not to do so. He will not take control of our lips and tongues. It is entirely up to each believer to move his lips and tongue and utter words that the spirit gives forth, just as in the mechanics of speech we use in our native language.

"interpretation of tongues"

Paul explains the manifestation of the interpretation of tongues in 1 Corinthians 14: "I wish you all spoke with tongues, but even more that you prophesied; for he who prophesies is greater than he who speaks with tongues, unless indeed he interprets, that the church may receive edification" [v.5, NKJV]. And in verse 13 he says: "Therefore let him who speaks in a tongue pray [believe] that he may interpret." And in verse 27 he says: "If anyone speaks [out loud] in a tongue [in a church service], let there be two or at the most three, each in turn, and let one [*heis*-the numeral one, and according to verses 5 and 13, "the same one"] interpret." The interpretation of tongues in a fellowship of believers is to be done by the same one who speaks in tongues out loud. The one who speaks in tongues must trust God to give him the interpretation in the language of the people present. The interpretation will not be a word-for-word translation of what was spoken in tongues; rather, it is simply the "gist" of what was spoken.

The manifestation of speaking in tongues is speaking to God and not to people. It is perfect praise for our Heavenly Father, exalting Him, magnifying Him, "giving thanks well" [1 Corinthians 14:17, NKJV]. Therefore, the manifestation of the interpretation of tongues will also be praise for our God. Speaking in tongues with the interpretation in a church service (or any fellowship of believers large or small) is primarily for the benefit of people (believers or those individuals merely curious) who are not mature in the Christian faith and may be unfamiliar with or skeptical of the manifestations of the spirit. "Therefore," Paul says, "tongues are for a sign, not to those who believe but to the unbelievers; but prophesying is not for unbelievers but for those who believe" [14:22].

"prophecy"

The manifestation of prophecy is the communication via the gift of holy spirit in a believer from God or the Lord Jesus Christ to another person or persons. The message may be verbal or written. The Bible itself is pure prophecy—"the testimony of Jesus is the spirit of prophecy" [Revelation 19:10, NKJV]. Prophecy may be "forth telling" or "foretelling the future." Most of the Bible is forth telling. Thus the manifestation of prophecy will, most of the time, be simply the forth telling of what is already revealed in the Bible, appropriate for the circumstantial needs of the person or persons for whom it is intended. The manifestation of prophecy in a church service will edify, exhort and comfort [1 Corinthians 14:3] the believers present. Rarely will there be any foretelling the future in the manifestation of prophecy, for that is the responsibility of one who has the gift ministry of a prophet [Ephesians 4:11], although a message of exhortation may give the person or persons for whom it is intended guidance and confidence to believe in the promises of God. The manifestation of prophecy can reveal the secrets of people's hearts [1 Corinthians 14:24,25] and inspire them to seek God.

Bringing a message from the Lord to His people by means of the manifestation of prophecy is not only a wonderful privilege for everyone born of the spirit, it is important for the well being of the Body of Christ. That's why Paul was inspired by the Lord to say: "Pursue love, and desire spiritual *gifts* [*gifts* is in italics in the KJV and NKJV here and also in 1 Corinthians 13:2 because it is not in the Greek text. Read: "things of the spirit"], but especially that you may prophesy" [1 Corinthians 14:1, NKJV]. And also: "Therefore, brethren, desire earnestly [*zeloo*-"be zealous"] to prophesy and do not forbid to speak with tongues" [14:39]. And also: "Do not quench the Spirit. Do not despise prophecies" [1 Thessalonians 5:19,20, NKJV].

False prophets and false prophecies are common among God's people [Jeremiah 14:14, Matthew 7:15, 1 John 4:1]. A genuine manifestation of prophecy will always be in alignment and harmony with the word of God and never contrary to it. Thus it behooves God's people to know God's word and to be taught it consistently in our churches and fellowship groups so that the people are not confused or deceived but receive the edification, exhortation and comfort God intends for His people.

"word of knowledge"

The manifestation of the word [*logos*-"decree, conception, message"] of knowledge is information given by the Lord to a believer which the believer cannot know or discover by means of his five senses. The Lord provides the message—not a single word but rather a concept or idea—via the believer's spirit and his spirit reveals it to his understanding. A word of knowledge may be made known to a believer in a variety of ways. The believer may instantly see a picture in his mind or hear the "still small voice" of the Lord or feel a telling sensation in his body or simply experience a strong emotion giving him understanding of what the Lord is communicating via his spirit. Most of the time, for a mature believer who has been faithfully "walking by the spirit," the information comes in the form of an instantaneous "knowing" what the Lord wants him to understand.

Along with our Heavenly Father's revelation of Himself and His ways with His people revealed in the Bible, the manifestations of the word of knowledge and the word of wisdom are the primary ways He communicates with His children.

"word of wisdom"

The manifestation of the word of wisdom normally accompanies the manifestation of the word of knowledge. A word of wisdom is revelation from the Lord to a believer's spirit letting him know *what to do* about the information given in a word of knowledge. It is spiritual guidance or direction. Sometimes a word of wisdom is not necessary along with the word of knowledge because w*hat to do* about the information provided is apparent. Proverbs 1:6 says: "For the Lord gives wisdom; from His mouth comes knowledge and understanding" [NKJV]. And Proverbs 4:7: "Wisdom is the principal thing; therefore get wisdom. And in all your getting, get understanding." Great wisdom and understanding of life comes from studying God's Word. A word of wisdom to a believer gives him understanding, that is, *what to do* regarding the *specific* information or circumstances revealed to him by the Lord in a word of knowledge.

A great teacher of God's people once said that the manifestations of the word of knowledge and the word of wisdom are the "eyes and ears" of the Church, the Body of Christ. Believers who learn to operate and become adept at and comfortable with these manifestations will be a great blessing to the local church in intercessory prayer, corporate and personal prophecy, the discerning of spirits, and in the laying on of hands for the ministering of miracles and gifts of healing because the Lord gives understanding of spiritual challenges beyond what we can know by means of our five senses. Paul tells us in Hebrews 5:14: "But solid [spiritual] food is for the mature, for those who have their powers of [spiritual] discernment trained by constant practice to distinguish good from evil" [ESV]. As a believer matures in the Lord, he learns to discern and distinguish revelation from the Lord from his own thoughts and feelings.

Sometimes information from the Lord via our spirit comes through clearly and distinctly because the Lord wants to be sure we don't miss it. For example, Peter's vision on the housetop when he "saw the heavens opened and something like a great sheet descending" was a message the Lord did not want him to miss, for this "happened three times, and the thing was taken up at once to heaven" [Acts 10:11,16, ESV]. Yet most of the time the revelation comes as a whisper or a "still small voice" which can easily be drowned out by the "noise" of the world bombarding us constantly from television, loud music or chatter on the radio, street noise, anger, arguments, even illness. God says: "Be still and know that I am God" [Psalm 46:10]. Believers must learn how to "be still" in our minds and souls. We can't always shut out the noise of the world around us, but we can perseveringly "edify" our spirit by speaking in tongues much so as to be ready to receive information from the Lord in times of need. Speaking in tongues much strengthens our spirit so that we are more readily able to discern the "still small voice" of the Lord distinctly.

Our Heavenly Father desires to communicate and commune with His children and will always provide the understanding and wisdom we need to deal with any situation if we will ask Him for it. "If any one of you lacks wisdom," James says, "let him ask God who gives generously to all without finding fault, and it will be given him" [James 1:5, NKJV].

"discerning of spirits"

The manifestation of the discerning of spirits is not what some teachers say is "discernment." It is not natural perception or insight. The manifestation of the discerning of spirits is revelation from God or the Lord Jesus Christ to our spirit regarding the presence or non-presence of spirits—whether holy spirit or unholy spirits [demons]—and our spirit reveals it to our understanding. The information revealed may include the identity of the spirit or spirits present and whether or not we may cast them out by the power of God in Christ in us [*dunamis*] and the authority we have in the name of Jesus Christ.

Ephesians 6:10-12 tells believers to "be strong in the Lord and in the strength [*dunamis*] of His might. Put on the whole armor of God, that you may be able to stand against the schemes of the devil. For we do not wrestle against flesh and blood, but against the rulers, against the authorities, against the cosmic powers over this present darkness, against the spiritual forces of evil in the heavenly places" [ESV]. God informs us that there are many spirits at work in society including angels and unholy spirits, as well as holy spirit in believers. By means of the manifestation of the discerning of spirits, believers can discern whether or not a person we might be praying for or ministering to is born of the spirit of God or is oppressed by a demon or demons and what to do about the situation— whether or not we may cast out the demon—or do nothing. Sometimes as we are laying on hands for ministering to a person, the wisdom we receive from the Lord may inform us not to cast out the demon at that time because in God's word Jesus teaches: ". . . when an unclean spirit goes out of a man, he [it] goes through dry places seeking rest, and finds none. Then he says, 'I will return to my house from which I came.' And when he comes, he finds it empty, swept, and put in order. Then he goes and takes with him seven other spirits more wicked than himself, and they enter and dwell there; and the last state of that man is worse than the first" [Matthew 12:43-45; Luke 11:24-26, NKJV]. When ministering to an individual, it may be necessary to discern from the Lord whether or not that person is willing to be taught to obey the Lord and change a lifestyle that allowed "unclean spirits" to oppress him—that is, how to stand against the demons and keep them out—before the demons can be cast out.

The manifestation of the discerning of spirits works *in process* with the manifestations of word of knowledge and word of wisdom. Indeed, depending on the situation and guidance from the Lord, it may also work *in process* with the manifestations of believing faith, miracles, and gifts of healing. If believers are to deal effectively with the reality of "the cosmic powers over this present darkness, against the spiritual forces of evil in the heavenly places," then we must learn to operate the manifestation of the discerning of spirits. Our Heavenly Father beseeches us to be "praying at all times in the Spirit, with all prayer and supplication . . ." [Ephesians 6:18, ESV]. Only by doing what God instructs and beseeches us to do can we remain "in touch" with how the Lord is leading us in triumph day by day.

"believing faith"

The manifestation of [believing] faith is not simple faith in God or the Lord Jesus Christ or that the Bible is true and reliable. The biblical definition of "faith"—*pistis* in the Greek—is "trust," and believers learn to trust God and to trust God's word only after God has proven Himself to us by honoring the promises in His word. Proverbs

3:5 says: "Trust in the Lord with all your heart, and do not lean on your own understanding" [ESV]. And Hebrews 11:1 says: "Faith is the assurance of things hoped for, the conviction of things not seen" [ESV]. However, the manifestation of faith is absolute trust regarding a *specific situation* revealed to the believer by means of a word of knowledge and/or a word of wisdom or the discerning of spirits. In other words, it is the believer's *absolute conviction* that what God or the Lord Jesus Christ has revealed to him will *certainly come to pass* when he acts on the revelation. As well, the manifestation of believing faith may be an *ongoing* process of trust—no matter how long it takes—for a specific revelation to a believer. For example, God told Abraham, by means of a word of knowledge: "'Look now toward heaven, and count the stars if you are able to number them . . . So shall your descendants be.' And he [Abraham] believed the Lord, and He counted it to him as righteousness" [Genesis 15:5,6, NKJV]. And Romans 4 tells us that Abraham "who, contrary to hope, in hope believed, so that he became the father of many nations, according to what was spoken, 'So shall your descendants be.' And not being weak in faith, he did not consider his own body, already dead (since he was about a hundred years old), and the deadness of Sarah's womb. He did not waver at the promise of God through unbelief, but was strengthened in faith, giving glory to God, and being fully convinced that what He had promised He was also able to perform" [Romans 4:18-21, NKJV].

Thus the manifestation of believing faith can be contrasted with simple faith. It is the specific faith necessary to accomplish the specific tasks or opportunities God or the Lord Jesus Christ asks us to accomplish. We cannot do miracles or impart gifts of healing by our own human ability. We must receive revelation from God or the Lord Jesus Christ by means of a message of knowledge and/or a message of wisdom or the discerning of spirits, and then by acting in *complete faith* on the revelation, bring to pass the miracle or healing, in the name of Jesus Christ, by means of the power [*dunamis*] inherent in us.

"miracles"

1 Corinthians 12:10 tells us that the working of miracles is given to believers and is energized by "the one and the same Spirit," that is, the gift of holy spirit born in each believer. The word "workings" in

the Greek text can be properly translated "energizing" or "effecting" because the manifestation of the working of miracles results in the evidencing or "clear display" of holy spirit energy in a given situation. The "working" or "performing" of miracles requires the operation of several manifestations of the spirit *in process*. It requires revelation from God or the Lord Jesus Christ via the manifestations of a message of knowledge, a message of wisdom, discerning of spirits depending on the situation, and the manifestation of absolute believing faith for the believer to act upon what he has been guided to do in order to bring to pass, that is, "energize" the miracle. Moreover, the manifestation of the working of miracles requires maturity in Christ. In order to muster the believing faith that the Lord will absolutely activate the energy to effect the miracle, a believer must be "walking by faith, not by sight" in his everyday life, meditating on the word of God daily, and speaking in tongues much in order to edify the spirit so as to hear "the still, small voice" of God.

God demonstrates in His word that miracles are available to faithful believers and should be happening in the Body of Christ regularly as the need arises. Miracles demonstrate the presence and power of God in our lives and build our faith for more and more of the promises of God to come to pass. As well, they demonstrate the ineffable love of God to heal and deliver His people, as Acts 10:38 says: ". . . how God anointed Jesus of Nazareth with the Holy Spirit and with power. He went about doing good and healing all who were oppressed by the devil, for God was with Him" [NKJV]. Believers represent the Lord Jesus Christ in our communities. The spirit—the anointing—of God in Christ is born in us, and we are enabled and encouraged by our Heavenly Father to walk "in demonstration of the Spirit and of power," as Paul expressed to the Corinthians, "that your faith might not rest in the wisdom of men but in the power of God" [1 Corinthians 2:4,5, NKJV].

"gifts of healing"

Like the manifestation of the working of miracles, the manifestation of gifts of healing requires the operation of several manifestations of the spirit *in process* including a message of knowledge, a message of wisdom, the discerning of spirits depending on the situation, the manifestation of believing faith, and the manifestation of the working of miracles.

Indeed, instantaneous healing is a miracle. The manifestation of gifts of healing is the culmination of a spiritual process of information revealed to the believer's spirit by the Father or the Lord Jesus Christ who activates the power [*dunamis*] in the believer as he or she acts in faith on the revelation.

Prior to His ascension into heaven to be with His Father, Jesus told His disciples: ". . . you will receive [*lambano*-"receive into evidence by taking it"] power [*dunamis*] when the Holy Spirit has come upon you, and you will be my witnesses in Jerusalem and in all Judea and Samaria, and to the end of the earth" [Acts 1:8, ESV]. Every born-again believer in Christ has the gift of holy spirit within and the potential power promised by the Lord. By reason of their trusting in the Lord, as well as their biblical education and experiential walk with the Lord, some believers may excel in the operation of the manifestation of gifts of healing, just as some may excel in the manifestation of the working of miracles or the manifestation of prophecy. However, it's clear from the word of God that all believers in Christ have the inherent potential to operate all of the manifestations of the spirit according to their understanding and faith to do so.

God heals in many ways. The psalmist informs us that we are "fearfully and wonderfully made" [Psalm 139:14, ESV]. Natural healing is built into the divinely- designed human body. Restorative healing may result over time according to the steadfast faith of the believer so that healing may be realized without the operation of the manifestation of the gifts of healing. Intercessory prayer may lead to healing. God tells believers to "pray for one another that you may be healed. The prayer of a righteous person has great power as it is working" [James 5:16, ESV]. However, when believers are ministering to one another by the laying on of hands, once we have thanked God for the revelation necessary for the effective ministering to the individual's needs, we must boldly act on what the Lord directs us to do and step out in absolute trust. No doubt many more believers would be operating the manifestations of the working of miracles and gifts of healing if they understood the spiritual process involved and truly believed that the Lord will work in them to "set at liberty those who are oppressed" [Luke 4:18b, ESV].

An important note: Paul concludes his discussion of *pneumatikos* with an injunction: "If anyone thinks himself to be a prophet or spiritual, let him acknowledge that the things I write to you [here in these statements] are the commandments of the Lord. But if anyone is ignorant, let him be ignorant" [1 Corinthians 14:37, 38, NKJV]. There is no "magic formula" to the operation of the manifestations of the spirit. God's grace, God's love for us, God's timing is everything. Indeed, when it comes to the manifestations of miracles and gifts of healing, it is entirely up to the Lord to "grant signs and wonders to be done" by the hands of faithful believers. Acts 14:3 informs us that Paul and Barnabas, while in Iconium, "stayed there a long time, speaking boldly in the Lord, who was bearing witness to the word of His grace, granting [*didomi*-"to give, supply, furnish, deliver"] signs and wonders to be done by their hands" [NKJV]. The Lord does the "granting"—"supplying, furnishing" authority by means of the manifestations of the spirit. We cannot do the signs, miracles and wonders on our own authority. Nevertheless, it is important and vital that we, as the children of God, do our best to study, to learn, to "grow up into Him who is the head"—Christ Jesus—and to be prepared for the love and power of our Heavenly Father to be manifested in our lives. "Therefore lift your drooping hands and strengthen your weak knees, and make straight paths for your feet, so that what is lame may not be put out of joint but rather be healed" [Hebrews 12:12,13, ESV].

Summary
"Now concerning *pneumatikos . . ."*

The Lord does not want His people to be ignorant concerning "the things of the spirit"—*pneumatikos.* Therefore He provides detailed information regarding "diversities of gifts," "differences of ministries," and "diversities of activities," but makes it clear that "the manifestation of the spirit is given to each one for the profit of all."

Verse to Remember: "I would like every one of you to speak in tongues" [1 Corinthians 14:5, NIV].

Question to ask Myself: If Jesus said I *could,* and Paul said I *should,* who am I to say I can't?

Exercise: Speak in tongues much. Remind yourself by putting "SIT" notes on the dash of your car, on your bathroom mirror, on your computer monitor, etc. Even if you've been speaking in tongues for years, praise Him in the spirit more and more.

SIX

The Lord's Curriculum

In his letter to the Ephesians, Paul makes known what the Lord Jesus Christ revealed to him regarding God's Plan for the Ages: ". . . making known to us the mystery of his will, according to his purpose which he set forth in Christ as a plan for the fullness of time, to unite all things in him, things in heaven and things on earth . . . so that in the coming ages he might show the immeasurable riches of his grace in kindness toward us in Christ Jesus" [Ephesians 1:8-10, 2:7, ESV]. As well, here in Ephesians and elsewhere in Paul's letters to the Church of the Body of Christ, the Lord reveals the gist of His "curriculum" of study, field experience, and spiritual preparation for the members of His Body of which He is the head. Paul says: "To me, though I am the very least of all the saints, this grace was given, to preach to the Gentiles the unsearchable riches of Christ, and to bring to light for everyone what is the plan of the mystery hidden for ages in God who created all things, so that through the church the manifold wisdom of God might now be made known to the rulers and authorities in the heavenly places" [Ephesians 3:8-10, ESV].

Too few Christians are even aware that our Lord Jesus Christ has prescribed a specific curriculum of study and practice for the members of His Body with the purpose being to guide us into becoming transformed more and more into His glorious likeness. The benefits of being steadily transformed into His likeness are, of course, wonderful! As we build ourselves up on our most holy faith [Jude 20], not only are we energized and encouraged to do the works that Jesus did in His earthly ministry—"and greater works than these,"—we also have the unspeakable reward of one day seeing Him "face to face" and being fully transformed into His likeness when He returns for us at the Rapture of the Church and, ultimately at the judgment seat of Christ, receiving the rewards of our faithful service that will last throughout eternity.

Webster's Collegiate Dictionary defines "curriculum," in its general sense, as "a set of courses constituting an area of specialization." "Curriculum" comes to us from the Latin meaning "running course." In his letter to the Galatians, Paul charges the believers: "You were running well. Who hindered you from obeying the truth? This persuasion is not from Him who calls you" [Galatians 5:7,8, ESV]. As believers progress in "the Lord's curriculum," we find ourselves "running well"— "specializing" in becoming more and more like Him. For some Christians it can be a rocky road if they don't follow teachers who faithfully present God's word in its integrity and accuracy. Many churches and seminaries focus their teaching programs on the four Gospels and the Old Testament, failing to "rightly handle" the Scriptures for the Body of Christ. In 2 Timothy 2:15 Paul says "Do your best to present yourself to God as one approved, a worker who has no need to be ashamed, rightly handling the word of truth" [ESV]. The Amplified Bible says it this way: "Study and be eager and do your utmost to present yourself to God approved (tested by trial), a workman who has no cause to be ashamed, correctly analyzing and accurately dividing (rightly handling and skillfully teaching) the word of Truth." The fact is, the four Gospels and the Old Testament were designed by God and written down "for our learning"—for the members of Christ's Body to learn from and understand all that God has done in preparing us for our times. Paul writes in Romans 15:4: "For whatever was thus written in former days [that is, prior to the Age of God's Grace which began at Pentecost] was written for our instruction, that by (our steadfast and patient) endurance and the encouragement (drawn) from the Scriptures we might hold fast to and cherish hope" [AMP]. The NKJV says: "For whatever things were written before were written for our learning . . . ." The Gospels and the Old Testament contain essential information for the born-again believer to know and understand regarding God's dealing with humanity and His preparing the Children of Israel to bring forth the Messiah—the Redeemer—and regarding the ministry of His Son, Jesus Christ, in bringing many sons to salvation. And yet it is in the New Testament [technically the Gospels conclude the Old Testament prophesies of the coming Redeemer] and specifically in the letters of Paul to the various churches, where our Lord reveals His systematic curriculum of study and practice so that the members of His Body may become like Him. Churches which focus most of their teaching and preaching on the Gospels and the Old Testament may very well inspire and educate their people as to what "came before," but they will never help believers to become "changed"—"transformed"—into the Lord's likeness. That's what "the Lord's curriculum"—revealed to Paul by Jesus Himself—is for. Paul testifies: "But I make known to you, brethren, that the gospel [euaggelion-"the glad tidings of the kingdom of God soon to be set up"] which was preached by me is not according to man. For I neither received it from man, nor was I taught it, but it came through the revelation of Jesus Christ" [Galatians 1:11,12, NKJV]. And in the epitome of his revelation from the Lord regarding the Great Mystery of the Body of Christ, Paul declares to the Ephesians that "He [Christ Jesus] is our peace who has made us [Jew and Gentile] both one [spiritually], and has broken down in his flesh [by His sacrifice on the cross] the dividing wall of hostility by abolishing the law of commandments expressed in ordinances, that he might create in himself one new man in place of the two, so making peace, and might reconcile us both to God in one body through the cross, thereby killing the hostility. And he came and preached peace to you [Gentiles] who were far off and peace to those who were near [Jews]. For through him we both have access in one Spirit [the gift] to the Father. So then you are no longer strangers and aliens, but you are fellow citizens with the saints [all believers] and members of the household of God, built on the foundation of the apostles and prophets, Christ Jesus himself being the cornerstone, in whom the whole structure, being joined together, grows into a holy temple [the Body of Christ] in the Lord. In him you also are being built together into a dwelling place for God by the Spirit" [Ephesians 2:14-22, ESV].

This is the Great Mystery revealed—the hidden counsel that the Lord revealed to Paul to preach to the members of His Body: ". . . assuming that you have heard of the stewardship of God's grace [the Administration of Grace] that was given to me [by the Lord] for you, how the mystery [mysterion-"secret counsel"] was made known to me by revelation, as I have written briefly. When you read this you can perceive my insight into the mystery of Christ, which was not made known to the sons of men in other generations as it has now been revealed to his holy apostles and prophets by [dia-"through or by means of"] the Spirit. This mystery is that the Gentiles are fellow heirs, members of the same body, and partakers of the promise in Christ Jesus through the gospel" [Ephesians 3:2-6, ESV].

Paul continues to exhort the members of the Body of Christ: "I, therefore, a prisoner of the Lord, urge you to walk in a manner worthy of the calling to which you have been called, with all humility and gentleness, with patience, bearing with one another in love, eager to maintain the unity of the Spirit in the bond of peace. There is one body and one Spirit—just as you were called to the one hope that belongs to your call—one Lord, one faith, one baptism, one God and Father of all, who is over all and through all and in all. But grace was given to each one of us according to the measure of Christ's gift . . . And he gave the apostles, the prophets, the evangelists, the shepherds and teachers, to equip the saints for the work of the ministry, for building up the body of Christ, until we all attain to the unity of the faith and of the knowledge of the Son of God, to mature manhood, to the measure of the stature of the fullness of Christ, so that we may no longer be children, tossed to and fro by the waves and carried about by every wind of doctrine, by human cunning, by craftiness in deceitful schemes. Rather, speaking the truth in love, we are to grow up in every way into him who is the head, into Christ, from whom the whole body, joined and held together by every joint with which it is equipped, when each part is working properly, makes the body grow so that it builds itself up in love" [Ephesians 4:1-7, 11-16, ESV].

God's fervent desire is that each member of the Body of Christ learn to "work properly" so that the whole Body is built up in love. The NIV says: "as each part does its work." And the Message Bible says: "God wants us to grow up, to know the whole truth and tell it in love—like Christ in everything. We take our lead from Christ, who is the source of everything we do. He keeps us in step with each other. His very breath and blood flow through us, nourishing us so that we will grow up healthy in God, robust in love."

God has given us the information we need—the guidelines, the revelation—so that each member of the Body of Christ can learn and understand his or her specific role in the Body in order to "grow up in everyway into him who is the head" and, in so doing, help to build up the whole Body in the love of God. This is "the Lord's curriculum" for the members of His Body. "The Lord's curriculum" may be presented in three sections: 1) Renewing our mind; 2) Praying without ceasing; and 3) Putting off the old self and putting on the new, including the whole armor of God.

Renewing our mind

When a person confesses out loud Jesus Christ as Lord and believes in his heart that God raised Him from the dead, the Bible says [Romans 10:9] he is "saved" [*sozo*-"rescued from destruction"]. At that moment he becomes "a new creation. The old has passed away, behold, the new has come" [2 Corinthians 5:17]. This is his time of commencement—a new way of life, a new beginning: "For you [your old self] have died," Paul says in Colossians 3, "and your life is hidden with Christ in God" [v. 3, ESV]. The new believer becomes "a new creation" in Christ and yet he still has the mind of his old self. He must begin the process of renewing his mind in order to "Let this mind [*phroneo*-"attitude, way of thinking"] be in you which was also in Christ Jesus" [Philippians 2:5, NKJV].

Jesus said: "For I have come down from heaven, not to do my own will, but the will of Him who sent me" [John 6:38, ESV]. If we are to learn to do the will of our Heavenly Father in every area of our lives, we need to let the attitude and way of thinking of the Lord, who is the head of the Body, become our attitude and way of thinking. Paul writes in Romans 12:2: "Do not be conformed [*syschematizo*-"fashion one's self to another's pattern"] to this world, but be transformed [*metamorphoo*-"changed, transfigured"] by the renewal [*anakainosis*-"renovation, new in quality, complete change for the better"] of your mind [*nous*-"intellectual faculties of perceiving, understanding, judging; faculty of perceiving divine things"] that by testing you may discern what is the will of God . . ." [ESV]. As the believer renews his mind to the word of God, he experiences a process of transforming his thinking and his attitudes from the deceitful patterns of the world to the truth of God's word. This is not a physical transformation; rather it's a transformation of attitude, understanding and character, although the physical "metamorphosis" of a crawling caterpillar into a beautiful butterfly that flies away into the sky is a fascinating figure. The objective of the believer's transformation—or "metamorphosis"—is to become like Christ in mind and attitude and, ultimately, "when He is revealed, we shall be like Him, for we shall see Him as He is" [1 John 3:2,

NKJV]. Thus we too shall one day "fly away"—"to meet the Lord in the air" [1 Thessalonians 4:17]. Proverbs 4 instructs us: "My son, be attentive to my words; incline your ear to my sayings. Let them not escape from your sight; keep them within your heart [lebab-"inner man, soul, conscience"]. For they are life to those who find them, and healing to all their flesh. Keep your heart with all vigilance, for from it flow the springs of life" [4:20-23, ESV]. After the death of Moses, God instructed Joshua: "This Book of the Law shall not depart from your mouth, but you shall meditate [hagah-"muse, mutter, devise, speak"] in it day and night, that you may observe to do according to all that is written in it. For then you will make your way prosperous, and then you will have good success" [Joshua 1:8, NKJV].

Clearly it's vital to read and study the Scriptures faithfully in order to renew one's mind to the living word of God—the attitudes and way of thinking of our Lord Jesus Christ. But simply reading and studying is not enough to effect "transformation." A believer might memorize many scripture verses without ever fully comprehending their spiritual depth and meaning. Only when the knowledge of God's word truly affects and cleanses his "heart"—which is the "inner man"—his "soul"—does his mind become "new in quality," completely changed for the better. This takes time and discipline, but genuine believing emanates from the believer's heart—the innermost part of his mind [nous]—and not from mental assent. Believing God's word from the heart is what facilitates the demonstration of the power [dunamis] and authority [exousia] of "Christ in you," as the Lord gives us guidance.

Indeed, Paul, by way of wisdom from the Lord, has much to say about the proper attitude and way of thinking for the faithful believer. In Romans 8 he says: "those who live according to the flesh [the old nature] set their minds on the things of the flesh, but those who live according to the Spirit [the new self] set their minds on the things of the Spirit. For to set the mind on the flesh is death [vain, empty—no spiritual reward], but to set the mind on the Spirit is life and peace. For the mind that is set on the flesh is hostile to God, for it does not submit to God's law; indeed, it cannot. Those who are in the flesh cannot please God" [Romans 8:5-8, ESV]. Moreover, he says in Galatians 5: "I say then: Walk [peripateo-"progress, regulate one's life"] in the Spirit, and you shall not fulfill the lust of the flesh. For the flesh lusts against the Spirit, and the Spirit against the flesh; and these are contrary to one another, so that you do not do the things that you wish" [vss. 16-17, NKJV]. The Amplified Bible is more emphatic in its conclusion to verse 17: "so that you are not free but are prevented from doing what you desire to do." The new believer has a desire in his spirit to do the will of the Lord, but if he is lax in renewing his mind to the word of God and therefore allows the old nature's attitude and way of thinking to rule him, he may want to accomplish good things on behalf of the Lord, but he is *prevented* from doing so because he ends up serving the desires of his old nature rather than the desires of his spirit. This is a sad fact for many Christians who have not been taught the importance of renewing their minds—or even if they have been taught, are lax in working at it—in order to be changed more and more into a spirit-led, victorious believer.

"the lamp of your body"

"Your eye is the lamp of your body," Jesus teaches in Luke 11. "When your eye is healthy, your whole body is full of light, but when it is bad, your body is full of darkness" [v. 34, ESV]. The Lord's use of synonyms is marvelous. The "eye" is the "lamp" of the body. The "lamp" allows the "light" to shine forth. The "eye" represents one's thinking, attitude, understanding, conscience and focus. When one's focus is "healthy," that is, on the things of God, one's "whole body"—or being—is full of "light"—the presence of God. When one's thinking and focus is "bad" ["For all that is in the world—the desires of the flesh and the desires of the eyes and pride in possessions . . ." [1 John 2:16, ESV]]— your body is full of darkness. Therefore be careful lest the light in you be darkness. If then your whole body [being] is full of light [illuminated by God's presence and purpose], having no part dark, it will be wholly bright, as when a lamp with its rays gives you light" [vss. 35,36.]. This is the purpose of "the Lord's curriculum" for the members of His Body—that our whole being may be full of light, the presence of God.

Paul has more to say about the importance of believers renewing their minds in relationship to other members of Christ's Body. In Philippians 1:27 he says: "Only let your conduct be worthy of the gospel of Christ, so whether I come and see you or are absent, I may hear of your affairs, that you stand fast in one spirit, with one mind [*psyche*-"breath, life force"] striving together for the faith of the gospel" [NKJV]. And in Philippians 2:2, NKJV, he says: "fulfill my joy by being like-minded [*autos*-"the same"], having the same love, being of one accord [*sympsychos*-"of one mind, harmonious"], of one mind [*phroneo*-"attitude"]. In 1 Corinthians 1:10, NKJV, he writes: "Now I plead with you, brethren, by the name of our Lord Jesus Christ, that you all speak the same thing, and that there be no divisions among you, but that you be perfectly joined together in the same mind [*nous*-"intellectual faculty, understanding, capacity for spiritual truth"] and in the same judgment [*gnome*-"mind, reason, opinion"]. And in Ephesians 4 he says: ". . . put off your old self, which belongs to your former manner of life and is corrupt through deceitful desires, and to be renewed in the spirit of your minds [*nous*], and to put on the new self created after the likeness of God in true righteousness and holiness" [vss. 22,23, ESV]. In any fellowship of believers, it is vital that the whole Body be of "one mind," "striving together for the faith of the gospel," so that the prayers and desires and goals of the whole Body are not hindered. Thus it behooves every individual believer to strive for the ongoing renewal of his mind to the word of God, "for we are members of one another" [Ephesians 4:25b, NKJV].

"No other doctrine"

In his letters to his protégé Timothy, Paul becomes even more focused and insistent regarding "the Lord's curriculum" for the members of His Body. In 1 Timothy 1:3, ESV, he says: "As I urged you when I went into Macedonia—remain in Ephesus that you may charge some that they teach no other doctrine . . ." [*heterodidaskaleo*-"deviating from the truth"]. Then in verse 10 he refers to the "sound doctrine" [*hygiaino didaskilia*-"error free teaching, instruction"] according to the blessed God which was committed to my trust." Here Paul is reminding Timothy that the doctrine—the teaching, instruction—which he received by revelation from the Lord is the only sound doctrine "of the glorious gospel [good news] of the blessed God" which must be taught and believed. We are reminded that in Galatians 1 Paul declares: ". . . I make known unto you, brethren, that the gospel which was preached by me is not according to man. For I neither received it from man, nor was I taught it, but it came through the revelation [word of knowledge and word of wisdom] of Jesus Christ." Paul's defense of his doctrine comes after he charges the believers in Galatia that "I marvel that you are turning away so soon from Him who called you in the grace of Christ, to a different gospel, which is not another, but there are some who trouble you and want to pervert the gospel of Christ. But even if we, or an angel from heaven, preach any other gospel to you than what we have preached to you, let him be accursed. As we have said before, so now I say again, if anyone preaches any other gospel to you than what you have received, let him be accursed" [vss. 6-9, NKJV]. This is heady stuff indeed! Paul affirms emphatically that the revelation he received from the Lord Jesus Christ and which he was preaching and teaching to the believers everywhere, and contained in his letters to all of the churches of the Body of Christ, was the *only sound doctrine* for faith and practice, and that Christian teachers were to teach *no other doctrine.* And in his final instructions to the believers in Rome, he says: "I appeal to you, brothers, to watch out for those who cause divisions and create obstacles contrary to the doctrine that you have been taught; avoid them. For such persons do not serve our Lord Christ, but their own appetites, and by smooth talk and flattery they deceive the hearts of the naïve" [Romans 16:17, ESV].

Furthermore, in 1 Timothy 4:1 Paul says: "Now the Spirit [the gift in him] expressly says [via word of knowledge and word of wisdom from the Lord] that in latter times some will depart from the faith, giving heed to deceiving spirits and doctrines of devils" [NKJV]. But he encourages Timothy in verse 6b: "If you instruct the brethren in these things, you will be a good minister of Jesus Christ, nourished in the words of faith and of the good doctrine [sound teaching] which you have carefully followed." Again he exhorts: "Until I come, give attention to reading, to exhortation, to doctrine;" and also: "Take heed to yourself and to the doctrine, for in doing this you will both save [*sozo*-"keep sound, rescue from danger"] yourself and those who hear you" [vss. 13 and 16].

To Titus Paul writes: "For an overseer [*episcopos*-"elder, bishop, guardian"], as God's steward, must be above reproach . . . He must hold firm to the trustworthy word as taught, so that he may be able to give instruction in sound doctrine [*hygiaino didaskalia*-"good health;" metaphorically "of Christians whose opinions are free from any mixture of error;" "teaching, instruction"]. Again he says to Titus: "But as for you, teach what accords with sound doctrine" [*hygiaino didaskalia*].

In his second letter to Timothy, Paul writes: "Hold fast the pattern of sound words which you have heard from me . . . ;" also: "And the things that you have heard from me among many witnesses, commit these to faithful men who will be able to teach others also" [2 Timothy 1:13, 2:2, NKJV]. In his final days in prison in Rome, aware that his time is running out, he writes these urgent words to his faithful son in the faith with an emphasis on the teaching and preservation of the sound doctrine which the Lord had revealed to him to teach to the faithful: "But know this, that in the last days perilous times will come: For men will be lovers of themselves, lovers of money, boasters, proud, blasphemers, disobedient to parents, unthankful, unholy, unloving, unforgiving, slanderers, without self-control, brutal despisers of good, traitors, headstrong, haughty, lovers of pleasure rather than lovers of God, having a form of godliness but denying its power. And from such people turn away!" [3:1-5, NKJV]. He continues: "But you have carefully followed my doctrine, manner of life, purpose, faith, longsuffering, love, perseverance, persecutions, afflictions," he says in verses 10 and 11. And finally he says: "I charge you therefore before God and the Lord Jesus Christ, who will judge the living and the dead at His appearing and His kingdom: Preach the word! Be ready in season and out of season. Convince, rebuke, exhort, with all longsuffering and teaching. For the time will come when they will not endure sound doctrine, but according to their own desires, because they have itching ears, they will heap up for themselves teachers; and they will turn their ears away from the truth, and be turned to fables" [2 Timothy 4:1-4, NKJV]. Prophetically, in our times, many churches and so-called Christian organizations have "turned their ears away from the truth" of the "sound doctrine" Paul received from the Lord, and they have turned aside to fables, preferring to hold fast to religious tradition and new-age philosophy in contradiction to the truth of "the Lord's curriculum." Thus it is vital that every faithful believer in Jesus Christ strive to study the word of God and renew his mind to the truths contained therein, so as not to be conformed [syschematizo-"fashioned, conformed to pattern"] to this world, but "be transformed by the renewal of your mind, that by testing you may discern what is the will of God, what is good and acceptable and perfect."

Praying without ceasing

Along with the renewal of one's mind according to the word of God, equally vital to becoming more like Christ is the Lord's appeal to believers in 1 Thessalonians 5:16-18: "Rejoice always, pray without ceasing, give thanks in all circumstances; for this is the will of God in Christ Jesus for you" [ESV]. The Amplified Bible is more insistent: "Be unceasing in prayer (praying perseveringly); Thank (God) in everything (no matter what the circumstances may be, be thankful and give thanks), for this is the will of God for you (who are) in Christ Jesus (the Revealer and Mediator of that will)." As well, in Ephesians 6:18, Paul says: ". . . praying always with all prayer and supplication in the Spirit, being watchful to this end with all perseverance and supplication for all the saints" [NKJV]. And in Hebrews 13:15 he says: "Through him [Jesus] let us continually [*diapantos*-"always"] offer up a sacrifice of praise to God, that is, the fruit of our lips that acknowledge his name" [ESV].

Why is it so important for believers to "pray without ceasing"—to pray "perseveringly?" And how is it even possible? Many believers don't realize that God is not in control of everything that happens on this earth. In fact, if God is in control of everything and that everything that happens—good or bad—is the will of God and happens for a reason, as many people believe, why pray at all if it doesn't make any difference in what happens? One little known verse in the Bible explains much: "We know that we [believers] are of God, and the whole world lies under the sway of the wicked one" [1 John 5:19, NKJV]. Indeed, in Ephesians 6 Paul beseeches believers to "be strong in the Lord and in the strength of his might. Put on the whole armor of God, that you may be able to stand against the schemes of the devil. For we do not wrestle against flesh and blood, but against the rulers, against the authorities, against the cosmic powers over this present darkness, against the spiritual forces of evil in the heavenly places" [6:12, ESV]. Not everything that happens in this world is God's doing; rather, "this present darkness" in every way is the result of the direct or indirect influence of "the wicked one." Fortunately, Colossians 1:3 informs believers that God "has delivered [rescued] us from the domain of darkness and transferred us to the kingdom of his beloved Son . . ." [ESV]. But that doesn't mean that believers in Christ get a "free pass" out from among the evil of this world. Believers need to "put on the whole armor of God" *in order* to be able to stand against the schemes of the devil. Standing against the schemes of the devil takes knowledge, wisdom, faith, and commitment.

In this vein, Romans 8:28 has been poorly translated in some versions of our Bibles and therefore misunderstood. The NKJV says: "And we know that all things work together for good to them that love God . . . ." Some have interpreted this to mean that since all things work together for good, then God must be responsible for and in charge of all things. But this is not what this scripture means. The NIV translates this verse: "And we know that *in all things* [italics supplied] God works for the good of those who love him . . . ." God will work to bring deliverance and victory to a believer in any situation—even if the situation is under the "sway" of "the wicked one" or by a chance of bad luck—according to the believer's desire for His help. That's why God urges us to "pray without ceasing"—to pray "perseveringly." The Bible teaches us that God does not have *carte blanche* to intervene in our lives and circumvent the evil that is everywhere. If He did, by His very nature—which is love, light, righteousness, justice and mercy—He would constantly be doing so. But we know from experience that this is not the world we live in. The devil is the "god of this world" [2 Corinthians 4:4, NKJV] and the director of "the rulers of this age" [1 Corinthians 2:6,8]. How did the devil get this dominion? Genesis 1:26, NKJV: "Then God said, 'Let Us make man in Our image, according to Our likeness; let them have dominion over the fish of the sea, over the birds of the air, and over the cattle, over all the earth* and over every creeping thing that creeps on the earth." The Scofield Study Bible, NKJV, includes an asterisk and notation regarding the phrase "over all the earth." It says: "Syriac reads *all the wild animals of.*" In the beginning God gave Adam dominion authority over fish, birds, cattle and "every creeping thing." Thus Adam's dominion over the earth was limited. When Adam committed high treason against God by his disobedience, this limited authority that he exercised was transferred to God's arch enemy, the devil, who reminds Jesus when he took Him "up on a high mountain, showed Him all the kingdoms of the world in a moment of time," and "said to Him: 'All this authority I will give you, and their glory; for this has been delivered to me, and I give it to whomever I wish'" [Luke 4:5,6, NKJV].

In the Greek the word "delivered" in this verse is *paradidomi*, meaning "to give over into one's power." Moreover, the Bible refers to the devil as "the prince of the power [*exousia*-"authority, liberty of doing what one pleases"] of the air" [*aer*-"lower atmospheric region"] [Ephesians 2:2, NKJV]. Regarding the devil's influence over this earth, in a revelation to Ezekiel, God says: "You [Lucifer] were in Eden, the garden of God; every precious stone was your covering . . . ; You were the anointed cherub who covers . . . ; You were perfect in your ways from the day you were created, till iniquity was found in you . . . ; Therefore I cast you as a profane thing out of the mountain of God . . . ; I cast you to the ground, I laid you before kings, that they might gaze at you" [Ezekiel 28:13a, 14a, 15, 16b, 17b, NKJV]. When the devil was "cast . . . to the ground" [*shalak*-"hurled, thrown down"]—to this earth—he carried with him authority as "the prince of the power of the air." In time he acquired the authority Adam transferred to him over created life as well. Thus 1 John 5:19, NKJV, tells us: "We know that we are of God, and the whole world [*kosmos*-"order, government, aggregate of things earthly"] lies *under the sway of* [*keimai*-"covered, lies in the power of"] the devil." And because God cannot act unrighteously—even toward the devil—He cannot circumvent the authority of the devil *unless* He is given the legal right to do so. Thus it is critical for God's people to "pray perseveringly." God needs our prayers in order to act on our behalf and bring to pass His will for our safety in this world and deliverance from the authority of the devil. Every son and daughter of God has been given the legal right and authority to pray in the name of Jesus Christ and thereby *invite* God and our Lord Jesus Christ and the angels of His power to intervene in "this present darkness" and bring deliverance to God's people.

Philippians 2:6 informs us that Jesus "who, though he was in the form of God, did not count equality with God a thing to be grasped" [ESV] [*harpagmos*-"act of seizing, robbery"—as when Lucifer attempted to seize control of heaven—Isaiah 14:12-14]. But, verses 8-11 say: "He humbled Himself and became obedient to the point of death, even the death of the cross. Therefore God has highly exalted Him and given Him the name which is above every name, that at the name of Jesus every knee should bow, of those in heaven, and of those on earth, and of those under the earth, and that every tongue should confess that Jesus Christ is Lord, to the glory of God the Father" [NKJV]. Every believer in Christ has been given the authority to use the name of Jesus Christ—"the name which is above every name"—for good. Colossians 3:17 says: "And whatever you do in word or deed, do all in the name of the Lord Jesus, giving thanks to God the Father through Him" [NKJV]. John assures us in his first letter: "And this is the confidence that we have toward him, that if we ask anything according to his will he hears us. And if we know that he hears us in whatever we ask, we know that we have the requests that we have asked of him" [1 John 5:14, 15, ESV]. And James declares: "Is anyone among you suffering? Let him pray. Is anyone cheerful? Let him sing praise. Is anyone among you sick? Let him call for the elders of the church, and let them pray over him, anointing him with oil in the name of the Lord. And the prayer of faith will save [*sozo*-"rescue, heal, restore"] the one who is sick, and the Lord will raise him up. Therefore, confess your sins to one another and pray for one another, that you may be healed. The prayer of a righteous person ["the earnest (heartfelt, continued) prayer"-AMP] has great power as it is working. Elijah was a man with a nature like ours, and he prayed fervently that it might not rain, and for three years and six months it did not rain on the earth. Then he prayed again, and heaven gave rain, and the earth bore its fruit" [James 5:13-18, ESV].

Praying effectually

Believers must learn to pray effectually. Ritual prayers have no place in God's heart. Jesus says: "And when you pray, do not use vain repetitions as the heathen do. For they think that they will be heard for their many words. Therefore, do not be like them" [Matthew 6:7, 8a, NKJV]. For the members of the Body of Christ, Philippians 4 gives guidelines for effectual prayer: "Do not fret or have any anxiety about anything, but in every circumstance and in everything, by prayer and petition (definite requests), with thanksgiving, continue to make your wants known to God. And God's peace (shall be yours, that tranquil state of a soul assured of its salvation through Christ, and so fearing nothing from God and being content with its earthly lot of whatever sort that is, that peace) which transcends all understanding shall garrison and mount guard over your hearts and minds in Christ Jesus" [vss. 6,7, AMP]. As well, Paul writes in 1 Timothy: "First of all, then, I urge that supplications, prayers, intercessions, and thanksgivings be made for all people, for kings and all who are in high positions, that we may lead a peaceful and quiet life, godly and dignified in every way" [2:1,2, ESV]. "Supplications" [*deesis*] are "needs, wants, entreaties through lack of personal resources." "Prayers" [*proseuche*] are all "earnest requests." "Intercessions" [*enteuxis*] means "a meeting with, falling in with God, often in behalf of others." In Luke 18:1 Jesus says: people "ought always to pray and not lose heart" [ESV]. The AMP says: "not faint, lose heart, give up." In other words, believers ought to "pray perseveringly." In Matthew 7, Jesus explains what it means to "pray perseveringly:" "Keep on asking and it will be given you; keep on seeking and you will find; keep on knocking (reverently) and (the door) will be opened to you. For everyone who keeps on asking receives; and he who keeps on seeking finds; and to him who keeps on knocking (the door) will be opened" [7:7, 8, AMP].

Essentially, prayer is simple communion with our Heavenly Father and with our Lord. Proverbs 3:5,6: "Trust in the Lord with all your heart, and do not lean on your own understanding. In all your ways acknowledge him, and he will make straight your paths" [ESV]. The scripture says "in all your ways acknowledge him." In other words, "whatever you do in word or deed, do all in the name of the Lord Jesus." This takes practice and dedication.

To "pray without ceasing" is to practice the presence of God. James says: "Draw near to God and He will draw near to you" [4:8, NKJV]. Practicing the presence of God enables us to overcome the darkness of the times. "In this world you will have tribulation," Jesus told His disciples. "But take heart; I have overcome the world" [John 16:33, ESV]. Jesus overcame the world when obediently He went to the cross to pay for the sins of the whole world [John 1:19: "Behold, the Lamb of God who takes away the sin of the world"] and God raised Him from the dead. By our faith in Christ, believers have overcome the world [system]: "For everyone who has been born of God overcomes the world [*kosmos*-"the aggregate of things earthly"]. And this is the victory that has overcome the world—our faith" [1 John 5:4, ESV]. "Our faith" has "overcome the world" because, spiritually, "God has made us alive with him" [Christ]: "And you, who were dead in your trespasses and uncircumcision of your flesh, God made alive together with him, having forgiven us all our trespasses, by canceling the record of debt that stood against us with its legal demands. This he set aside, nailing it to the cross. He disarmed the [spiritual] rulers and authorities and put them to open shame, by triumphing over them in him" [Colossians 2:13-15, ESV]. "For in him [Christ] the whole fullness of deity dwells bodily, and you have been filled [*pleroo*-"made complete, fully furnished"] in him who is the head of all rule and authority. In him also you were circumcised with a circumcision made without hands, by putting off the body of the flesh, by the circumcision of Christ, having been buried with him in baptism, in which you were also raised with him through faith by the powerful working of God, who raised him from the dead" [vss. 9-12, ESV]. God sees every born-again believer as having been crucified with Christ, buried with Him in baptism, raised from the dead to resurrection life, raised up and seated with Him "with every spiritual blessing in the heavenly places" [Ephesians 1:3, ESV]. Thus the believer's authority on the earth and over the world system in the name of Jesus Christ is phenomenal! In Luke 8, when a windstorm came down on the lake and endangered His disciples, "Jesus awoke and rebuked the wind and the raging waves, and they ceased and there was a calm. He said to them, 'Where is your faith?' And they were afraid, and they marveled, saying to one another, 'Who then is this, that he commands even wind and water, and they obey him?'" [vss. 24,25, ESV]. Jesus exercised authority over "even wind and water." Colossians 1:27 says to every born-again believer: "Christ in you, the hope of glory." And 1 John 4:17 declares: "By this is love perfected with us, so that we may have confidence for the day of judgment, because *as he is* [italics supplied] so also are we in this world" [ESV]. Indeed, in our spiritual potential, born-again believers also exercise authority over "wind and water," according to our persevering prayer and the Lord's granting signs and wonders via the manifestations of the spirit.

Knowing, then, why God encourages believers to "pray without ceasing," we cultivate the habit. "Draw near to God and He will draw near to you." We draw near to God simply by acknowledging His presence in everything we do or say. Most importantly, we "pray without ceasing" by praying in the spirit—speaking in tongues much. We know from the Scriptures that speaking in tongues is speaking "mysteries" to God, that it is speaking "the wonderful works of God," that it "magnifies God," and that it is "giving thanks well." Moreover, Paul informs us that speaking in tongues "edifies" our spirit. The truth is, our spirit must be edified everyday. Simply renewing our minds to God's word daily is not enough. We need also to be able to listen intuitively to God communicating with our spirit which our spirit then communicates to our perceptions, whether hearing, seeing, tasting, touching, feeling—or simply "knowing." God says: "Be still, and know that I am God." And in 1 Kings: ". . . after the wind an earthquake, but the Lord was not in the earthquake. And after the earthquake a fire, but the Lord was not in the fire. And after the fire the sound of a low whisper" [vss. 11,12, ESV]. The NKJV says: "a still small voice." The NIV: "a gentle whisper." The NASV: "a gentle blowing." The Darby: "a soft gentle voice." Speaking in tongues much edifies our spirit so that we are able to perceive the "soft gentle voice" of our Heavenly Father communicating with our spirit. In doing so we are "building [ourselves] up on [our] most holy faith." We are strengthening our faith in the promises of God so that we can truly "trust in the Lord with all [our] heart" more and more each day, not leaning on our own understanding, but acknowledging Him "in all [our] ways," so that He can "make our paths straight."

Put on the new self

Along with faithfully renewing our minds to the word of God so as to "let this mind be in you which was also in Christ Jesus," and speaking in tongues much in order to edify our spirit and thereby building ourselves up in faith, it's vital that the believer who desires to become a true disciple of the Lord learn to "put off" the old nature and "put on" the new. Paul gives details as to how this can be progressively accomplished: ". . . assuming that you have heard about him [Christ] and were taught in him, as the truth is in Jesus . . . put off your old self, which belongs to your former manner of life and is corrupt through deceitful desires, and . . . be renewed in the spirit of your minds, and . . . put on the new self, created after the likeness of God in true righteousness and holiness" [Ephesians 4:21-24, ESV]. Putting off "the old self" is best accomplished by putting on "the new self" since focusing on the positive is more encouraging than focusing on the negative. However, as we focus on the positive—on what God says who we are in Christ Jesus and on this grace wherein we stand—the negatives of our old nature become glaringly apparent. "Let no one deceive you with empty words," Paul says, "for because of these things the wrath of God comes upon the sons of disobedience [unbelievers]. Therefore do not become partners with them; for at one time you were darkness, but now you are light in the Lord. Walk as children of light (for the fruit of light is found in all that is good and right and true), and try to discern what is pleasing to the Lord. Take no part in the unfruitful works of darkness, but instead expose them. For it is shameful even to speak of the things that they do in secret. But when anything is exposed by the light, it becomes visible, for anything that becomes visible is light. Therefore it says, 'Awake, O sleeper, and arise from the dead, and Christ will shine on you'" [Ephesians 5:6-14, ESV]. Ephesians is written to believers in the Lord, not to unbelievers. So when Paul says "Awake, O sleeper," he is addressing believers who are "asleep at the switch" spiritually. When he says "arise from the dead," he means "get up out of the dead practices of the old self."

"God is light," 1 John 1:5 says, "and in him is no darkness at all. If we say we have fellowship with him while we walk in darkness, we lie and do not practice the truth. But if we walk in the light, as he is in the light, we have fellowship with one another, and the blood of Jesus Christ his Son cleanses us from all sin" [ESV]. Indeed, Christians are supposed to reflect the light of "Christ in you, the hope of glory." We do so as we practice righteous living. "For God, who said, 'Let light shine out of darkness,' has shone in our hearts to give the light of the knowledge of the glory of God in the face of Jesus Christ" [2 Corinthians 4:6, ESV]. "And we all, with unveiled face [unlike Moses who had to put a veil over his face as he stood before the Children of Israel—Exodus 34] beholding the glory of the Lord [in the word of God], are being transformed into the same image from one degree of glory to another. For this comes from the Lord who is the Spirit" [1 Corinthians 3:18, ESV]. We are being changed day by day—if we faithfully renew our minds to the word of God, speak in tongues much, and put on the "new self"—because it is a process of transformation into the Lord's glorified likeness—into the likeness of His *character* in this present life and into His metaphysical likeness when we see Him "face to face."

Light dispels darkness. This "transformation" from our old self to the new— because we are "putting on" light in the Lord—dispels the darkness of our old self so that we can perceive and understand just what we need to "put off" in order to become more like Christ. In his first letter to the Corinthians, Paul writes: "Do you not know that the unrighteous [*adikos*-"unjustified"] will not inherit the kingdom of God?" [1 Corinthians 6:9, NKJV]. Some teachers of the Bible say that it is possible to lose one's salvation by "backsliding" and practicing the unrighteous behavior listed in 1 Corinthians 6:9 and 10. But Paul is not talking about believers here. He's talking about the "unrighteous"—the unjustified. All born-again believers are made righteous in Christ—"justified by faith" [Romans 5:1]. Our righteousness and justification by faith are permanent [Romans 10:4; 2 Corinthians 5:21]. But the point is, there is no reward at the judgment seat of Christ for unrighteous behavior. Some believers will suffer the loss of rewards and be put to shame because of unrighteous behavior if the sin is not confessed and repented of [1 Corinthians 3:14,15; 1 John 1:9]. The Message Bible puts it more efficaciously: "Don't you realize that this is not the way to live? Unjust people who don't care about God will not be joining in his kingdom. Those who use and abuse each other, use and abuse sex, use and abuse the earth and everything in it, don't qualify as citizens in God's kingdom. A number of you know from experience what I'm talking about, for not so long ago you were on that list. Since then, you've been cleaned up and given a fresh start by Jesus, our Master, our Messiah, and by our God present in us, our Spirit" [1 Corinthians 9:11, MSG]. Paul goes on to say: "All things are lawful for me, but not all things are helpful. All things are lawful for me, but I will not be enslaved by anything" [1 Corinthians 6:12, ESV]. The MSG renders verse 12: "Just because something is technically legal doesn't mean that it's spiritually appropriate. If I went around doing whatever I thought I could get by with, I'd be a slave to my whims."

"seek the things that are above"

Much of Colossians 3 deals with the specifics of "putting off the old" and "putting on the new." Paul says: "If then you have been raised with Christ, seek the things that are above, where Christ is, seated at the right hand of God. Set your mind on things that are above, not on things that are on the earth. For you have died, and your life is hidden with Christ in God. When Christ who is your life appears, then you also will appear with him in glory" [vss. 1-4, ESV]. The MSG puts it this way: "So if you're serious about living this new resurrection life with Christ, act like it. Pursue the things over which Christ presides. Don't shuffle along, eyes to the ground, absorbed with the things right in front of you. Look up, and be alert to what is going on around Christ—that's where the action is. See things from his perspective" [vss. 1,2].

Paul continues in Colossians 3: "Put to death therefore what is earthly in you: sexual immorality, impurity, passion, evil desire, and covetousness, which is idolatry. On account of these the wrath of God is coming. In these you too once walked, when you were living in them. But now you must put them all away: anger, wrath, malice, slander, and obscene talk from your mouth. Do not lie to one another, seeing that you have put off the old self with its practices and have put on the new self, which is being renewed in knowledge after the image of its creator. Here there is not Greek and Jew, circumcised and uncircumcised, barbarian, Scythian, slave, free; but Christ is all, and in all. Put on then, as God's chosen ones, holy and beloved, compassionate hearts, kindness, humility, meekness, and patience, bearing with one another and, if one has a complaint against another, forgiving each other, as the Lord has forgiven you, so you also must forgive. And above all these put on love, which bonds everything together in perfect harmony. And let the peace of Christ rule in your hearts, to which indeed you were called in one body, teaching and admonishing one another in all wisdom, singing psalms and hymns and spiritual songs, with thankfulness in your hearts to God. And whatever you do, in word or deed, do everything in the name of the Lord Jesus, giving thanks to God the Father through Him" [Colossians 3:5-17, NKJV].

If a believer in Christ faithfully practices these things—renewal of his mind to the word of God so as to "put on the mind of Christ," praying perseveringly in the spirit, and putting off the old self by putting on the new—he will be well on his way to understanding the "secret to holy spirit authority" and exercising the power of the Lord's promise in John 14:12: "Truly, truly, I say to you, whoever believes in me will also do the works that I do, and greater works than these will he do, because I am going to the Father" [ESV].

As well, Peter encourages all believers to prepare for the glory that shall be revealed in us: God "has granted to us his precious and very great promises, so that through them you may become partakers of the divine nature, having escaped from the corruption that is in the world because of sinful desire. For this very reason, make every effort to supplement your faith with virtue [arete-"moral excellence"], and virtue with knowledge, and knowledge with self-control, and self-control with steadfastness, and steadfastness with godliness, and godliness with brotherly affection, and brotherly affection with love [agape-"charity, benevolence"]. For if these qualities are yours and are increasing, they keep you from being ineffective and unfruitful in the knowledge of our Lord Jesus Christ. For whoever lacks these qualities is so nearsighted that he is blind, having forgotten that he was cleansed from his former sins. Therefore, brothers, be all the more diligent to make your calling and election sure [*bebaios*-"stable, fast, firm"], for if you practice these qualities you will never fall. For in this way there will be richly provided for you an entrance into the eternal kingdom of our Lord and Savior Jesus Christ" [2 Peter 1:4-11, ESV].

"Put on the whole armor of God"

"Finally," Paul writes to the Ephesians, "be strong in the Lord and in the strength of his might. Put on the whole armor of God, that you may be able to stand against the schemes of the devil. For we do not wrestle against flesh and blood, but against the rulers, against the authorities, against the cosmic powers over this present darkness, against the spiritual forces of evil in the heavenly places. Therefore take up the whole armor of God, that you may be able to withstand in the evil day ["this present darkness"], and having done all, to stand firm" [Ephesians 6:10-13, ESV].

Paul states unequivocally that the believer's struggle is with "the spiritual forces of evil" and not against flesh and blood, although we know that the spiritual forces of evil seduce, deceive, and sometimes demonize people in order to carry out the will of the wicked one. To stand against spiritual wickedness, believers need spiritual weapons. The spiritual forces of evil work "behind the scenes" of our senses perceptions. That's why God urges His people to "pray at all times in the spirit, with all prayer and supplication" [Ephesians 6:18a, ESV]. Praying "in the spirit" should always precede any actions we take so as to invite the Lord to guide us in our actions. Many times situations may be out of our control and all we can do is pray for the Lord to intervene. Thus when Paul says to "be strong in the Lord" and to "stand firm," he's writing to faithful believers who understand that perseverance in prayer is a prerequisite. And as we persevere in prayer, we have "the whole armor of God" clothing us to help us to stand firm in the struggle.

"the belt of truth"

"Stand therefore, having fastened on the belt of truth . . ." [v. 14a]. In Paul's day the soldier's belt anchored the rest of his armor and so, like the soldier's belt, the truth of God's word is the anchor and foundation of a Christian's life. In the Garden of Gethsemane, Jesus prayed to the Father for His friends: "Sanctify them in the truth; your word is truth" [John 17:17, ESV]. In our society the devil wages a constant campaign of lies against the truth of God's word. It is incumbent on the believer to "Be diligent to present yourself approved to God, a worker who does not need to be ashamed, rightly dividing the word of truth" [2 Timothy 2:15, NKJV]. When Jesus was in the wilderness for forty days, and tempted by the devil, His reply was: "It is written, 'Man shall not live by bread alone, but by every word that proceeds from the mouth of God'" [Matthew 4:4, NKJV]. "*It is written* . . . ." And He said: "If you abide in My words, you are My disciples indeed; and you shall know the truth, and the truth shall make you free" [John 8:31,32, NKJV]. The truth of God's word dispels the darkness of the devil's lies and sets people free.

"the breastplate of righteousness"

". . . and having put on the breastplate of righteousness . . ." [v. 14b]. The Roman soldier of Paul's time wore a breastplate to protect his vital organs. The breastplate of Paul's figure of speech is the believer's right standing with God—"the free gift of righteousness" [Romans 5:17]—which each believer enjoys because of Christ's finished work on the cross: "For He [God] made Him [Christ] who knew no sin to be sin for us, that we might become the righteousness of God in Him" [2 Corinthians 5:21, NKJV]. Believers are called to "follow after righteousness" [2 Timothy 6:11], which is righteous living as the result, and that God's word provides "instruction in righteousness" [2 Timothy 3:16]. The faithful believer enjoys the mercy of God when "a righteous man may fall [sin] seven times and rise again" [Proverbs 24:16, NKJV]; and that when we stumble in our Christian walk, "If we confess our sins, He is faithful and just to forgive us our sins and to cleanse us from all unrighteousness" [1 John 1:9, NKJV]. We know, then, that we are forgiven and do not allow guilt or shame to drag on us and keep us from getting back to living righteously and standing firm against the schemes of the devil.

"the gospel of peace"

". . . and, as shoes for your feet, having put on the readiness given by the gospel of peace" [v. 15]. "Peace" is a "fruit of the spirit," the tranquility of the soul—of the mind and heart—which the faithful believer has put on as readiness against the onslaughts and schemes of the enemy because he knows his salvation in Christ is secure and that "God is our refuge and strength, a very present help in trouble" [Psalm 46:1, NKJV]. In Colossians 3:15, Paul urges believers to "let the peace of God rule in your hearts" [NKJV]; and in Philippians 4:7 he says, ". . . and the peace of God, which surpasses all understanding, will guard your hearts and minds through Christ Jesus" [NKJV].

"the shield of faith"

"In all circumstances take up the shield of faith with which you can extinguish all the flaming darts of the evil one" [v. 16]. The shield *is* the believer's faith. It protects us from the blows of the enemy—but it does not keep the blows from coming. Faith is the believer's trust that our Father "will never leave [us] nor forsake [us]" [Hebrews 13:5b, NKJV]. Faith is our trust that in all circumstances our Heavenly Father has our best interests in mind. For He has said, "Trust in the Lord with all your heart, and lean not on your own understanding. In all your ways acknowledge Him, and He shall direct your paths" [Proverbs 3:5, NKJV]. Faith is the believer's shield because "faith is the assurance of things hoped for, the conviction of things not seen" [Hebrews 11:1, ESV]. We hope for the return of Christ which we have not yet seen but which is "an anchor of the soul" [Hebrews 19]. Our faith assures us that He is coming one day soon.

"the helmet of salvation"

". . . and take the helmet of salvation . . ." [v. 17a]. The "helmet of salvation" protects the believer's mind and heart from losing hope in the future because of the problems and pressures of the present. "For

God has not destined us for wrath, but to obtain salvation through our Lord Jesus Christ, who died for us that whether we are awake [living] or asleep [in Christ] we might live with him" [1 Thessalonians 5:9, ESV]. The Christian's future salvation is assured although not yet fully realized because "the creation waits with eager longing for the revealing of the sons of God. For the creation was subjected to futility, not willingly, but because of him who subjected it in hope that the creation itself will be set free from its bondage to corruption and obtain the freedom of the glory of the children of God. For we know that the whole creation has been groaning together in the pains of childbirth until now. And not only the creation, but we ourselves, who have the firstfruits of the spirit, groan inwardly as we wait eagerly for adoption as sons, the redemption of our bodies. For in this hope we were saved. Now hope that is seen is not hope. For who hopes for what he sees? But if we hope for what we do not see, we wait for it with patience" [Romans 8:19-25, ESV]. "For the Lord himself will descend from heaven with a cry of command, with the voice of an archangel, and with the sound of the trumpet of God. And the dead in Christ will rise first. Then we who are alive, who are left, will be caught up together with them in the clouds to meet the Lord in the air, and so we will always be with the Lord. Therefore encourage one another with these words" [1 Thessalonians 4:16-18, ESV].

"the sword of the spirit"

". . . and the sword of the Spirit, which is the word of God . . ." [v. 17b]. The word of God is a spiritual sword given to believers to use in our daily lives as we "wrestle" with "the rulers of the darkness" of this world. In His temptations in the wilderness, Jesus used His spiritual sword—the word of God—against the wiles of the devil: "It is written . . . it is written . . . ." The "sword of the Spirit" sets the captives free: "And they were all amazed and said to one another, 'What is this word? For with authority and power he commands the unclean spirits, and they come out!'" [Luke 4:36, ESV]. The "sword of the Spirit" cuts to the heart: "For the word of God is living and active, sharper than any two-edged sword, piercing to the division of soul and spirit, of joints and of marrow, and discerning the thoughts and intentions of the heart" [Hebrews 4:12, ESV]. The Christian is commanded by God to take the "sword of the Spirit" and use it not only as an offensive weapon to cut through spiritual darkness but also as a defensive one. "The entrance of your words gives light; it gives understanding to the simple" [Psalm 119:130, NKJV]. When the word of God becomes dominant in our thinking, it is a discerner [*kritikos*-"critic"] of the very thoughts and intentions of our hearts" and keeps us on the path of righteous judgment and righteous living. It helps us to stand against the schemes of the enemy by giving us understanding and proper discernment. The "sword of the Spirit" cuts through the darkness and exposes those things done "in secret" by the rulers of the darkness of this world. Paul says: "Take no part in the unfruitful works of darkness, but instead expose them. For it is a shame even to speak of the things that they do in secret. But when anything is exposed by the light [the word of truth], it becomes visible" [Ephesians 5:11-13, ESV].

The "sword of the Spirit," as it cuts through the darkness and exposes the lies of the deceiver, brings healing and deliverance to the hearers: "He sent His word and healed them, and delivered them from their destructions" [Psalm 107:20,NKJV]. Thus Paul exhorts his beloved Timothy—and all leaders in the Body of Christ—"I charge you, therefore before God and the Lord Jesus Christ, who will judge the living and the dead at His appearing and His kingdom: Preach the word! Be ready in season and out of season. Convince, rebuke, exhort, with all longsuffering and teaching" [2 Timothy 4:1,2, NKJV].

Summary
The Lord's Curriculum

In His word, our Heavenly Father has given us the guidelines we need so that each member of the Body of Christ can learn and understand his specific role in the Body in order to "grow up into Him who is the head." This is "the Lord's curriculum" of study and practice, including renewing our mind to the word of God, praying perseveringly, putting off the old nature and putting on the new, and putting on "the whole armor of God."

Verse to Remember: "Do not be conformed to this world, but be transformed by the renewal of your mind, that by testing you may discern what is the will of God, what is good and acceptable and perfect" [Romans 12:2, ESV].

Question to ask Myself: Am I progressing in "the Lord's curriculum," or am I allowing myself to be conformed to the patterns of this world?

Exercise: Read Paul's letters to the Church—Romans through 1 & 2 Thessalonians, as well as 1 & 2 Timothy—in several different versions of the Bible. Despite nuances in interpretation in the various versions, the light of Truth comes shining through in the main. This is the heart of "the Lord's curriculum." The Lord said: "When the Spirit of truth comes, he [it] will guide you into all the truth . . ." [John 16:13a].

Seven

"Did you receive the Holy Spirit when you believed?

The baptism in holy spirit is God's most wonderful gift to humanity. It is the love, the grace, the mercy of God overflowing: "But God, being rich in mercy, because of the great love with which he loved us, even when we were dead in our trespasses, made us alive together with Christ—by grace you have been saved [*sozo*-"rescued from destruction"]—and raised us up with him and seated us in the heavenly places in Christ Jesus . . ."[Ephesians 2:4-6,ESV]. When a person confesses with his mouth "Jesus is Lord" and believes in his heart that God raised Him from the dead, he is saved. Other scriptures confirm this truth: "And it shall come to pass that whoever shall call on the name of the Lord shall be saved" [Acts 2:21, NKJV]; and: ". . . when the kindness and the love of God our Savior toward man appeared, not by works of righteousness which we have done, but according to His mercy He saved us, through the washing of regeneration ["new birth, recreation"] and renewing ["complete change for the better"] of the Holy Spirit, whom He poured out abundantly through Jesus Christ our Savior . . ." [Titus 3:5-7, NKJV]. To "call on the name of the Lord" is a figure of speech. It does not mean mere verbal petition; rather, it is to believe that Jesus is Lord and to worship Him. As this phrase is used in other scriptures [Genesis 12:8; Psalm 99:6, others], it implies submission.

Therefore, when a person "calls on the name of the Lord," believing in his heart that God raised Him from the dead, he is saved—delivered from destruction—unto everlasting life: "For God so loved the world that He gave His only begotten Son, that whoever believes in Him should not perish [*apollymi*-"be destroyed, entirely abolished"] but have everlasting life" [John 3:16, NKJV]. At the precise moment a person is saved, he receives the baptism in holy spirit, for it is only the baptism in holy spirit that is the "washing of regeneration" so that he becomes a "new creation" in Christ [2 Corinthians 5:17, NKJV]. Moreover, Paul assures us that the moment we are saved we are baptized in holy spirit: "And you also were included in Christ when you heard the message of truth, the gospel of your salvation. Having believed, you were marked in him with a seal, the promised Holy Spirit, who is a deposit guaranteeing our inheritance until the redemption of those who are God's possession—to the praise of his glory" [Ephesians 1:13,14, NIV]. The Message Bible says it beautifully: "It is in Christ that you, once you heard the truth and believed it (this Message of your salvation), found yourselves home free—signed, sealed, and delivered by the Holy Spirit." Ephesians 4:30 confirms that this "seal" is permanent: "And do not grieve the Holy Spirit of God, by whom you were sealed for the day of redemption" [the Rapture of the Church] [ESV].

Some preachers talk about a "second work of grace," referring to the baptism in holy spirit. This is totally unscriptural. There is no suggestion in the Bible of a "second work of grace." At the moment a person hears enough of "the word of truth" to "call on the name of the Lord," he is "saved," which is to be baptized in holy spirit—"sealed with the Holy Spirit of promise" [Ephesians 1:13, NKJV]. This is the one and only work of God's gift of grace in a believer, and it is a "complete package"—everything the new believer needs to begin the process of becoming more and more like Christ. Paul says in Colossians 2: "For in Him [Christ] dwells all the fullness of the Godhead bodily; and you are complete [*pleroo*-"filled to the full"] in Him, who is the head of all principality and power" [vss. 9,10, NKJV]. If a born-again believer is "complete in Him"—"filled to the full"—then there is no more "filling" or work of grace required for him to become like Christ.

Because most Christians do not immediately speak in tongues when they are saved—baptized in holy spirit—it may seem to some that it takes a "second work of grace" to enable them to speak. But this is not what God's word teaches us. The Acts of the Apostles is the history of the early Christian Church—its rise and expansion—and provides us with illuminating lessons regarding the baptism in holy spirit. Paul told the Corinthian church: "I thank God I speak in tongues more than you all." When did Paul first speak in tongues? The Scriptures are not definite but we can speculate that he first spoke in tongues the hour he was ministered to by a faithful believer named Ananias. In Acts 9 the Lord instructed Ananias, a simple believer, to "Arise and go to the street called Straight, and inquire at the house of Judas for one called Saul of Tarsus, for behold, he is praying. And in a vision he has seen a man named Ananias coming in and putting his hand on him, so that he might receive his sight" [9:11, 12, NKJV]. At first Ananias resisted the Lord's instructions since he had heard of Saul's determination to thwart the expansion of the Church. But eventually he "went his way and entered the house; and laying his hands on him he said, 'Brother Saul, the Lord Jesus, who appeared to you on the road as you came, has sent me that you might receive your sight and be filled [*pletho*-"filled to overflowing"] with the Holy Spirit. Immediately there fell from his eyes something like scales, and he received his sight at once, and he arose and was baptized" [vss. 11-17, NKJV].

Throughout the New Testament several different Greek words are translated "filled" in our English versions of the Bible. Two key words are *pleroo,* meaning "filled to the full, to the brim," and *pletho* [from *pimplemi* which is a prolonged form of the primary verb *pletho*] which means "to be fulfilled, furnished, or filled to overflowing," as opposed to merely filled to the brim. When Ananias laid his hands on Saul and prayed for him, Saul was "filled to overflowing" with holy spirit. We'll discover in other records in Acts just what "filled to overflowing" indicates.

In Acts 8, prior to Paul's conversion, Simon the sorcerer saw something remarkable: "When the apostles in Jerusalem heard that Samaria had accepted [*dechomai*-"received favorably"] the word of God, they sent Peter and John to Samaria. When they arrived, they prayed for the new believers there that they might receive [*lambano*-"take possession, experience, receive into evidence for use"] the Holy Spirit, because the Holy Spirit had not yet come on any of them; they had simply been baptized in the name of Jesus. Then Peter and John placed their hands on them, and they received [*lambano*-"took possession of, received into evidence"] the Holy Spirit. When Simon saw that the Spirit was given at the laying on of the apostles' hands, he offered them money and said, 'Give me also this ability so that everyone on whom I lay my hands may receive [*lambano*] the Holy Spirit'" [8:14-19, NKJV].

When Peter and John arrived in Samaria, they found new believers who had been saved—baptized in holy spirit—but without there being any evidence of their having been baptized. It's apparent that in the record of the rise and expansion of the early Church, normally there was evidence when someone was baptized in holy spirit, and that's why the apostles in Jerusalem sent two pillars of the Church—Peter and John—to Samaria. Something was wrong. We know from Peter's powerful sermon in the temple square in Jerusalem on the Day of Pentecost that he told the people: "Repent, and let every one of you be baptized in the name of Jesus Christ for the remission of sins, and you shall receive [*lambano*-"take possession of, receive into evidence"] the gift of the Holy Spirit" [Acts 2:38, NKJV]. Thus, when Peter and John laid their hands on the new believers in Samaria, they *"lambanoed"* holy spirit—they manifested. That's what Simon saw.

In the Greek text two key words translated "receive" in our English Bibles are d*echomai* and *lambano*. *Dechomai* means "to receive favorably, accept, embrace." *Lambano* means "to take possession of, to receive into evidence for one's use." What was it exactly that Simon the sorcerer "saw" happen? This becomes clear in Acts 10 when we study the record of Peter's visit to the house of Cornelius.

"God shows no partiality"

"There was a certain man in Caesarea called Cornelius, a centurion of what was called the Italian Regiment, a devout man and one who feared God with all his household, who gave alms generously to the people and prayed to God always" [Acts 10:1,2, NKJV]. Cornelius had a clear vision from God, an angel informing him that his prayers were about to be answered. Following the angel's specific instructions, Cornelius sent two of his household servants to Joppa to find Peter. Peter also had a clear vision. While he was praying, he "saw heaven opened and an object like a great sheet bound at the four corners, descending to him and let down to the earth. In it were all kinds of four-footed animals of the earth, wild beasts, creeping things, and birds of the air. And a voice came to him, 'Rise, Peter; kill and eat.' But Peter said, 'Not so, Lord! For I have never eaten anything common or unclean.' And a voice spoke to him again a second time, 'What God has cleansed you must not call common' . . . This was done three times," the scripture says, and Peter "wondered within himself what this vision which he had seen meant" [vss. 11-17, ESV]. It was then that the servants whom Cornelius had sent arrived and explained to Peter that Cornelius had been divinely instructed to invite him to come and speak to them. The next day Peter went with them, but he took witnesses—"brethren from Joppa"—knowing he was on shaky religious grounds being a devout Jew going to the house of Gentiles. When he arrived at the house of Cornelius, Cornelius had assembled his "relatives and close friends" and rehearsed for Peter the details of his angelic vision, how the angel had instructed him to send for Peter who would come and speak to them "all the things commanded you by God" [v. 33b].

"Then Peter opened his mouth and said, 'In truth I perceive that God shows no partiality; but in every nation whoever fears Him and works righteousness is accepted by Him'" [vss. 34,35]. This was a moment of enlightenment for Peter. Finally he understood the meaning of his vision from the Lord—that God was calling out both Gentiles and Jews to Himself. Then, while Peter spoke to the household of Cornelius: ". . . how God anointed Jesus of Nazareth with the Holy Spirit and with power, who went about doing good and healing all who were oppressed by the devil, for God was with Him" [v. 38], as he continued to teach, "the Holy Spirit fell upon all those who heard the word. And those of the circumcision who believed [the witnesses] were astonished, as many as came with Peter, because the gift of Holy Spirit had been poured out on the Gentiles also. For they heard them speak with tongues and magnify God. Then Peter answered, 'Can anyone forbid water, that these should not be baptized who have received [*lambano*-"received into evidence"] the Holy Spirit just as we have?'" [vss. 44-47].

The evidence of the baptism in holy spirit was speaking in tongues. "All those who heard the word" were baptized and spoke in tongues. And in Acts 9, speaking in tongues is precisely what Simon "saw" when Peter and John laid their hands on the new believers in Samaria.

"Did you receive the Holy Spirit when you believed?"

Acts chapter 19 provides us with another insightful lesson regarding the baptism in holy spirit. "And it happened, while Apollos was at Corinth [Apollos had recently been in Ephesus teaching the believers "accurately the things of the Lord, though he knew only the baptism of John"—Acts 18:25, NKJV] that Paul, having passed through the upper regions, came to Ephesus. And finding some disciples, he said to them, 'Did you receive [*lambano*-"receive into evidence"] the Holy Spirit when you believed?' So they said to him, 'We have not so much as heard whether there is a Holy Spirit.' And he said to them, 'Into what then were you baptized?' So they said, 'Into John's baptism.'"

Herein is an important lesson regarding baptism. The baptism in holy spirit is the only baptism that results in "the washing of regeneration"—the New Birth—as Titus 3:5 informs us. With the baptism in holy spirit, a believer is "born again" and becomes a "new creation in Christ"—"behold, all things have become new" [2 Corinthians 5:17, NKJV]. The "baptism of John," that is, water, was a requirement of the Old Testament Law and could never effect a "washing of regeneration" of the individual. Indeed, in Peter's defense to the Jews in Jerusalem following his visit to the Gentiles, he declared: "Then I remembered the word of the Lord, how he said, 'John indeed baptized with water, but you shall be baptized with the Holy Spirit'" [Acts 11:16, NKJV].

Then Paul said to the believers at Ephesus, "John indeed baptized with a baptism of repentance, saying to the people that they should believe on him who would come after him, that is, on Christ Jesus." When they heard this, they were baptized in the name of the Lord Jesus. And when Paul had laid his hands on them, the Holy Spirit came upon them, and they spoke with tongues and prophesied. Now the men were about twelve in all" [19:4-7, NKJV].

In the early Church, it was a common occurrence for the baptism in holy spirit to be evidenced by spontaneous speaking in tongues and prophesying. Beginning with Pentecost, the baptism in holy spirit was always evidenced by an "overflowing:" "And suddenly there came a sound from heaven, as of a rushing mighty wind, and it filled [*pleroo*-"filled to the full"] the whole house where they were sitting. Then there appeared to them divided tongues, as of fire, and one sat upon each of them. And they were all filled [*pletho*-"filled to overflowing"] with the Holy Spirit and began to speak with other tongues as the Spirit gave them utterance" [Acts 2:2-4, NKJV]. Prior to His ascension into heaven to be with the Father, Jesus promised His disciples: "Behold, I send the Promise of My Father upon you; but tarry in the city of Jerusalem until you are endued [clothed] with power [*dunamis*-"inherent power"] from on high" [Luke 24:49, NKJV]. ". . . For John truly baptized with water, but you shall be baptized with the Holy Spirit not many days from now . . . you shall receive [*lambano*-"receive into evidence"] power [*dunamis*] when the Holy Spirit has come upon you; and you shall be witnesses to Me in Jerusalem, and in all Judea and Samaria, and to the end of the earth" [Acts 1:5,8, NKJV].

The baptism in holy spirit not only washes clean and "regenerates" the new believer spiritually, making him "a new creation in Christ," it "clothes" him with "power from on high" so that he can begin to do the works that Christ did in His earthly ministry—"and greater works than these will he do." The "greater works" certainly involves leading another person to the Lord and into the baptism in holy spirit—"born from above" as a "new creation" in Christ. This is something Jesus could not do because the gift of holy spirit was not poured out on believers until the Day of Pentecost. "And you shall be witnesses to Me . . . ," the Lord said. The baptism in holy spirit enables the believer to be an effective witness to the resurrection of Jesus Christ from the dead "to the ends of the earth." Nothing has changed God's purpose and provision in the Body of Christ since the Day of Pentecost for more than two thousand years.

Summary
"Did you receive the Holy Spirit when you believed?"

The Acts of the Apostles provides many valuable lessons regarding believers who were "filled to overflowing" when they were baptized in holy spirit. In all cases this "overflowing" was the manifestation of speaking in tongues and/or prophesying.

Verse to Remember: " . . . You shall receive power when the Holy Spirit has come upon you, and you shall be witnesses to Me . . . to the end of the earth" [Acts 1:8, NKJV].

Questions to ask Myself: Have I received holy spirit into evidence in my life since I first believed in Christ? Have I been "filled to overflowing?"

Exercise: At the proper time, ask your pastor or other trusted Christian friend to lay hands on you for the manifestation of the spirit—speaking in tongues or prophesying—or for the revelation of your unique ministry of service in the Body of Christ. "Here I am, Lord. Send me!" [Isaiah 6:8].

EIGHT

"Walk by the Spirit"

"**B**lessed [*esher*-"happy"] is the man who walks [*halak*-"proceeds, manner of life"] not in the counsel of the ungodly, nor stands in the path of sinners, nor sits in the seat of the scornful; But his delight is in the law of the Lord, and in His law he meditates day and night. He shall be like a tree planted by the rivers of water, that brings forth its fruit in its season, whose leaf also shall not wither; and whatever he does shall prosper" [Psalm 1:1-3, NKJV].

Thus the psalmist introduces the believer to the great treasure of wisdom in the Book of Psalms, focusing in the first Psalm on two vital keys to prospering in the Lord: 1) avoid the manner of life of the ungodly, of sinners, of the scornful, and 2) delight in the word of God and meditate [*hagah*-"muse, mutter, devise, speak, imagine"] in it day and night. And this is precisely the purpose of "the Lord's curriculum" for the members of His Body—to guide the faithful believer in the steps to "walking by the Spirit" and prospering in the Lord.

"Do you not know," Paul asks the Roman believers, "that all of us who have been baptized into Christ Jesus were baptized into his death? We were buried therefore with him by baptism into death, in order that, just as Christ was raised from the dead by the glory of the Father, we too might walk in newness of life" [Romans 6:3,4, ESV]. Paul says to the Colossians: "If then you have been raised with Christ, seek the things that are above, where Christ is, seated at the right hand of God. Set your minds on things that are above, not on things that are on the earth. For you have died, and your life is hidden in Christ in God. When Christ, who is your life appears, then you also will appear with him in glory" [Colossians 3:1-4, ESV]. What do these verses mean "you have died" and "we were baptized into his death"? And what does it mean to "walk in newness of life"? The Message Bible says: "Your old life is dead. Your new life, which is your real life—even though invisible to spectators—is with Christ in God" [Colossians 3:3]. We understand that when the scripture says "For you have died," it's a figure of speech and not literal. Paul says in Hebrews: "How much more will the blood of Christ, who through the eternal Spirit offered himself without blemish to God, purify [*katharizo*-"cleanse, purge"] our conscience from dead works to serve the living God" [9:14, ESV]. When a believer is "born again" of the spirit of God, he is spiritually "cleansed" because the "incorruptible seed" from the Father—the spirit born in him—is pure. Therefore when the Bible says that believers have been "baptized into his death" and "buried" with Him by "baptism into death," and then "raised with him through [our] faith in the powerful working of God" [Colossians 2:12, ESV], it's speaking of our "identification" with Christ in God's eyes who "raised us up with him and seated us with him in the heavenly places in Christ Jesus" [Ephesians 2:6, ESV]. When God says believers have been "raised . . . up with him and seated . . . with him in the heavenly places," this also is a figure of speech—the "prophetic perfect." We realize that we are still here on earth and have not yet been "raised up and seated with Him . . . ." However, this is so certain to come to pass in God's timing that He speaks of it as though it has already occurred. This figure of speech—the "prophetic perfect"—can be found in use many times in the Bible, especially in the Old Testament in reference to the promised Messiah (see Isaiah 53). In God's eyes we have forever become "one" with His Son. Then as we walk in this "newness of life," we discover that we're enabled and empowered by the spirit born in us, "For we are his workmanship created in Christ Jesus for good works, which God prepared beforehand, that we should walk in them" [Ephesians 2:10, ESV]. The scripture doesn't mean that because "we have died" that our old nature is literally dead and no longer has any influence over us. Mature Christians understand that this is not the case. Rather, it means that we have been spiritually "washed"—cleansed—of the old nature in God's eyes and enabled to make progress in "newness of life." A believer can choose to allow his old nature of sin and dead works—separation from God—to have influence over him, and many Christians do. But by a deliberate decision day by day to "put off the old nature" and "put on the new" by faithfully progressing in "the Lord's curriculum" of study and practice, we walk in "newness of life" more and more efficaciously. It's clear from Paul's encouragement to the believers in Thessalonika that walking in "newness of life" is not automatic once a person is saved: "Finally, then, brothers, we ask and urge you in the Lord Jesus, that as you received from us how you ought to walk and to please God, just as you are doing, that you do so more and more. For you know what instructions we gave you through the Lord Jesus. For this is the will of God, your sanctification [*hagiasmos*-"purification, effect of consecration"]: that you abstain from sexual immorality; that each one of you know how to control his own body in holiness and honor, not in the passion of lust like the Gentiles who do not know God; that no one transgress and wrong his brother in this matter, because the Lord is an avenger in all these things, as we told you beforehand and solemnly warned you. For God has not called us for impurity, but in holiness. Therefore whoever disregards this, disregards not man but God, who gives his Holy Spirit to you" [1 Thessalonians 4:1-8, ESV].

"But I say," Paul writes to the Galatians, "walk by the Spirit, and you will not gratify the desires of the flesh. For the desires of the flesh are against the Spirit, and the desires of the Spirit are against the flesh, for these are opposed to each other, to keep you from doing the things you want to do" [Galatians 5:16,17, ESV]. And to the Corinthians he says: "So we are always of good courage. We know that while we are at home in the [mortal] body, we are [physically] away from the Lord, for we walk by faith, not by sight" [2 Corinthians 5:6,7, ESV]. To "walk by faith" is to "walk by the Spirit," faithfully reading and studying God's word so as to "put on the mind of Christ," praying perseveringly for the Lord's wisdom; for God to work in us "both to will and to do for his good pleasure" [Philippians 2:13, ESV]; and for God's help as we "put off the old nature" and "put on the new." "For this is the message that we have heard from him and proclaim to you," John writes in his first letter, "that God is light and in him is no darkness at all. If we say we have fellowship [*koinonia*-"communion, participation"] with him while we walk in darkness [the old nature], we lie and do not practice the truth. But if we walk in the light, as he is in the light, we have fellowship with one another, and the blood of Jesus his Son cleanses us from all sin. If we say we have no sin, we deceive ourselves, and the truth is not in us. If we confess our sins, he is faithful and just to forgive us our sins and to cleanse us from all unrighteousness. If we say we have not sinned, we make him a liar, and his word is not in us" [1 John 1:5-10, ESV]. The MSG says it this way: "If we claim that we experience a shared life with him and continue to stumble around in the dark, we're obviously lying through our teeth—we're not living what we claim. But if we walk in the light, God himself being the light, we also experience a shared life with one another, as the sacrificed blood of Jesus, God's Son, purges all our sin" [1 John 1:5-7]. Therefore, John says, "whoever says he abides in him ought to walk in the same way in which he walked" [1 John 2:6, ESV]. And how did Jesus walk? He said: "My food is to do the will of him who sent me and to accomplish his work" [John 4:34, ESV]. Moreover, Peter declared to the household of Cornelius: ". . . how God anointed Jesus of Nazareth with the Holy Spirit and with power. He went about doing good and healing all who were oppressed by the devil, for God was with him" [Acts 10:38, ESV].

"be imitators of God"

To "walk by the spirit," which is to "walk by faith"—just as Abraham walked with God by faith, "for he endured as seeing him who is invisible" [Hebrews 11:27, ESV]—is to "walk in love." "Therefore be imitators of God, as beloved children," Paul writes to the Ephesians. "And walk in love, as Christ loved us and gave himself for us, a fragrant offering and sacrifice to God. But sexual immorality and all impurity or covetousness must not even be named among you, as is proper among saints. Let there be no filthiness nor foolish talk nor crude joking, which are out of place, but instead let there be thanksgiving. For you may be sure of this, that everyone who is sexually immoral or impure, or who is covetous (that is, an idolater), has no inheritance in the kingdom of Christ and God" [Ephesians 5:1-5, ESV]. What the Scriptures are pointing out here is that unconfessed sin of any nature cancels out spiritual rewards at the judgment seat of Christ following the Rapture of the Church. At that time, Paul says, "each of us will give an account of himself to God" [Romans 14:12, ESV]. "For we must all appear before the judgment seat of Christ, so that each one may receive what is due for what he has done in the body [in this mortal life], whether good or evil. Therefore, knowing the fear [*phobos*-"dread, reverence"] of the Lord, we persuade others" [2 Corinthians 5:10,11, ESV]. At the judgment seat of Christ, believers receive spiritual rewards for what we have done in this mortal life to love, to obey, and to serve the Lord. The quality and quantity of these spiritual rewards are being determined *here and now* by the quality of our Christian walk. For some, rewards will be cancelled out by sin not confessed and therefore not forgiven. "Each one's work will become manifest," Paul says, "for the Day will disclose it, because it will be revealed by fire, and the fire will test what sort of work each one has done. If the work that anyone has built on the foundation [Jesus Christ] survives, he will receive a reward. If anyone's work is burned up, he will suffer loss, though he himself will be saved, but only as through fire" [1 Corinthians 3:13-15, ESV]. But praise be to God, the psalmist says, "The Lord is merciful and gracious, slow to anger and abounding in steadfast love. He will not always chide, nor will he keep his anger forever. He does not deal with us according to our sins, nor repay us according to our iniquities. For as high as the heavens are above the earth, so great is his steadfast love to those who fear him; as far as the east is from the west, so far does he remove our transgressions from us. As a father shows compassion to his children, so the Lord shows compassion to those who fear him. For he remembers our frame; he remembers that we are dust" [Psalm 103:8-14, ESV].

Our Heavenly Father wants His children to "imitate" [*mimetes*-"follow"] Him and walk in love [*agape*] "as dear children" [Ephesians 5:1]. "God is love." "God is light and in Him is no darkness at all" [1 John 1:5, NKJV]. God is good, righteous, just, gracious, merciful, kind, and holy. His desire for us is that we strive to become like Him to the best of our ability in this mortal life. He will reward us for all eternity in His presence.

"And so," Paul writes to the Colossians, "from the day we heard [of your faith in Christ], we have not ceased to pray for you, asking that you may be filled with the knowledge of his will in all spiritual wisdom and understanding, so as to walk in a manner worthy of the Lord, fully pleasing to him, bearing fruit in every good work, and increasing in the knowledge of God" [1:9,10, ESV]. "Therefore," he continues, "as you received Christ Jesus the Lord, so walk in him, rooted and built up in him and established in the faith, just as you were taught, abounding in thanksgiving" [2:6,7, ESV]. "Walk in wisdom toward outsiders, making the best use of the time. Let your speech always be gracious, seasoned with salt, so that you may know how you ought to answer each person" [4:5,6, ESV].

All things considered in the word of God regarding walking by the spirit, it becomes obvious that it's possible to train ourselves to become more and more like Christ. Moreover, it's clear that the battlefield is in the mind. "Be transformed by the renewal of your mind [NKJV]," Paul exhorts. The AMP says: "Do not be conformed to this world (this age), [fashioned after and adapted to its external, superficial customs] . . . ." And the New Living Translation [NLT] says: "Don't copy the behavior and customs of this world, but let God transform you into a new person by changing the way you think. Then you will learn to know God's will for you, which is good and pleasing and perfect."

Indeed, by controlling what we think, we can actually "train" ourselves to be "godly." Paul writes to Timothy: "Have nothing to do with irreverent, silly myths. Rather train yourself for godliness; for while bodily training is of some value, godliness is of value in every way, as it holds promise for the present life and also for the life to come" [1 Timothy 4:7,8, ESV]. In the Greek the word for "train" is *gymnazo*, meaning "exercise vigorously, in any way, either the body or the mind." Paul says to the Corinthians: "Do you not know that in a race all the runners run, but only one receives the prize. So run that you may obtain it. Every athlete exercises self-control in all things. They do it to receive a perishable wreath, but we an imperishable. So I do not run aimlessly; I do not box as one beating the air. But I discipline my body and keep it under control, lest after preaching to others I myself should be disqualified" [1 Corinthians 9:24-27, ESV].

We might ask ourselves "What's *my* training program?" "Where do I need to grow spiritually? Am I faithfully reading and studying God's word, praying perseveringly, endeavoring to put off the old nature and to put on the new? Am I joining in fellowship with other like-minded believers, sharing my faith, and giving of my abilities and prosperity to help others when I can?" As well, "Am I casting my care on the Lord each new day, knowing that God is my sufficiency, not dwelling on past mistakes, disappointments or failures?" The scripture says: "forgetting what lies behind and straining forward to what lies ahead, I press on toward the goal of the prize of the upward call of God in Christ Jesus" [Philippians 3:13,14, ESV].

As for myself, I echo the words of the gifted evangelist David Wilkerson who said: "I have not yet fully arrived in this glorious walk—but I am gaining ground." And in the words of Paul who told the Philippians: "And I am sure of this, that he who began a good work in you will bring it to completion at the day of Jesus Christ" [Philippians 1:6, ESV].

"Finally, brothers," Paul says, "whatever is true, whatever is honorable, whatever is just, whatever is pure, whatever is lovely, whatever is commendable, if there is any excellence, if there is anything worthy of praise, think about these things. What you have learned and received and heard and seen in me—practice [*prasso*-"exercise, perform, accomplish"] these things, and the God of peace will be with you" [Philippians 4:8,9 ESV].

Summary
"Walk by the Spirit"

To "walk by the Spirit" is to "walk by faith," which is to "walk in love."

Verse to Remember: "Therefore be imitators of God, as beloved children. And walk in love, as Christ loved us and gave himself for us, a fragrant offering and sacrifice to God" [Ephesians 5:1,2, ESV].

Questions to ask Myself: Am I "in training" to be godly—exercising vigorously? Where can I do better?

Exercise: I will trust in the Lord with all my heart . . . I will acknowledge Him in all my ways. I will practice doing this. I will get better and better at it.

NINE

"The fruit of the Spirit"

"**H**ow am I doing, Lord?" We might ask Him this from time to time in our spiritual progress. Certainly the Lord will give us insight if we are being honest with Him and with ourselves and faithfully progressing in "the Lord's Curriculum," because "the word of God is living and powerful . . . and is a discerner [critic] of the thoughts and intents of the heart. And there is no creature hidden from His sight, but all things are naked and open to the eyes of Him to whom we must give account" [Hebrews 4:12,13, NKJV].

Indeed, our Heavenly Father has give His children a general standard by which we may gage, from time to time, our spiritual progress in the Lord. In Galatians 5, Paul, by way of the spirit, says: "Walk by the Spirit and you will not gratify the desires of the flesh," [5:16] and he delineates the works of the flesh. Then he says: "But the fruit [*karpos*-"advantage, profit, posterity, harvest"] of the Spirit is love, joy, peace, patience, kindness, goodness, faithfulness, gentleness, self-control; against such things there is no law. And those who belong to Christ have crucified the flesh with its passions and desires. If we live by the Spirit, let us also walk by the Spirit" [vss. 22-25, ESV].

"Therefore by their fruits you will know them," the Lord says [Matthew 7:20, NKJV]. "Even so, every good tree bears good fruit, but a bad tree bears bad fruit. A good tree cannot bear bad fruit, nor can a bad tree bear good fruit. Every tree that does not bear good fruit is cut down and thrown into the fire" [Matthew 7:17-19, NKJV]. Remarkably, in this context, the Lord warns of "false prophets, who come to you in sheep's clothing, but inwardly they are ravenous wolves. You will know them by their fruits" [vss. 15, 16a]. "Not everyone who says to me, 'Lord, Lord,' shall enter the kingdom of heaven, but he who does the will of

My Father in heaven. Many will say to Me in that day, 'Lord, Lord, have we not prophesied in Your name, cast out demons in your name, and done many wonders in Your name?' And I will declare to them, 'I never knew you; depart from Me, you who practice lawlessness'" [vss. 21-23]. By way of explanation, the Lord says: "A good man out of the good treasure of his heart [*kardia*-"soul, center of spiritual life"] brings forth good; and an evil man out of the evil treasure of his heart brings forth evil. For out of the abundance of the heart his mouth speaks" [Luke 6:45, NKJV].

Throughout history many deceivers of God's people have appeared in "sheep's clothing." Even today some who exalt themselves as apostles or prophets and publicly refer to Jesus as Lord and even prophesy in His name and cast out demons in His name and do wonders in His name are nevertheless counterfeit. Are they rightly-dividing the word of truth, teaching aspects of "the Lord's Curriculum" to their followers and edifying the Body of Christ in love? Or are they concerned primarily with self-promotion and self-aggrandizement? Paul says: "For we are not, like so many, peddlers of God's word, but as men of sincerity, as commissioned by God, in the sight of God we speak in Christ" [2 Corinthians 2:17, ESV].

In the Parable of the Sower, Jesus says: ". . . some seed fell on good ground, sprang up, and yielded a crop a hundredfold" [Luke 8:8, NKJV]. When His disciples asked Him to explain, He said: "The seed is the word of God . . . the ones that fell on the good ground are those who, having heard the word with a noble and good heart, keep it and bear fruit with patience" [8:11,15, NKJV].

The Lord wants the members of His Body to "bear fruit with patience." "I am the true vine, and My Father is the vine dresser," He instructs His disciples in John 15. "Every branch in Me that does not bear fruit He takes away; and every branch that bears fruit He prunes [*kathairo*-"cleans of impurity, metaphorically to expiate"], that it may bear more fruit. Abide in Me, and I in you. As the branch cannot bear fruit of itself, unless it abides in the vine, neither can you, unless you abide in Me. I am the vine, you are the branches. He who abides [*meno*-"remains, continues"] in Me, and I in him, bears much fruit; for without Me you can do nothing. If anyone does not abide in Me, he is cast out as a branch and is withered; and they gather them and throw them into the fire, and they are burned. If you abide in Me, and My words abide in you, you will ask what you desire, and it shall be done for you. By this My Father is glorified, that you bear much fruit; so you will be My disciples" [John 15:1-8,NKJV].

Paul writes to the Ephesians: "Let no one deceive you with empty words ["excuses, groundless arguments"—MSG], for because of these things the wrath of God comes upon the sons of disobedience. Therefore do not be partakers with them. For you were once darkness, but now are you light in the Lord. Walk as children of light, for the fruit ["result, harvest"] of the Spirit [some texts read "light"] is in all goodness, righteousness, and truth, finding out what is acceptable to the Lord" [Ephesians 5:6-10,NKJV].

Our Heavenly Father wants to be glorified in our lives as we "bear fruit with patience." And so He gives us guidelines by which we may ascertain our progress.

Love

Love, as a fruit of the spirit, is the ability to love like Jesus loved. "Beloved, let us love one another, for love is from God, and whoever loves has been born of God and knows God. Anyone who does not love does not know God, for God is love" [1 John 4:7,8, NKJV]. The word in the Greek text for the love that is from God is a*gape*. *Agape* love is a greater love than *phileo* ["affection, strong liking for someone"] or *eros* ["sexual or passionate love"]. *Agape* love is realized from the action it prompts: Jesus did not want to go to the cross, but "greater love has no man than this, that someone lay down his life for his friends" [John 15:13, ESV]. *Agape* love is a deliberate exercise of the will and not based on affection or emotion or liking someone. Only by means of *agape* love are we able to "love your enemies, bless those who curse you, do good to those who hate you, and pray for those who spitefully use you and persecute you, that you may be sons of your Father in heaven" [Matthew 5:44,45a, NKJV].

Agape love energizes our faith [Galatians 5:6] and prompts us to be "imitators of God as dear children. And walk in love, as Christ also has loved us and has given Himself for us" [Ephesians 5:1,2, NKJV]. *Agape* love enables us to see through the eyes of "Christ in you" and base our actions toward others on the love of Christ: "For the love of Christ compels us, because we judge thus: that if One died for all, then all died; and He died for all, that those who live should no longer live for themselves, but for Him who died for them and rose again" [2 Corinthians 5:14,15, NKJV].

"Whoever has my commandments and keeps them," Jesus says, "he it is who loves me. And he who loves me will be loved by my Father, and I will love him and manifest myself to him" [John 14:21, ESV]. *Agape* love is a maturing of the fruit of the spirit in a believer in his progress in becoming transformed more and more into the image of Christ.

Joy

"The joy of the Lord is your strength," Nehemiah declared to the people when the wall of Jerusalem had been rebuilt [Nehemiah 8:10]. And the "joy of the Lord" is still the strength of God's people today. In the Greek text the word for "joy" is *chara,* meaning "gladness." It is the strength of God's people in the sense of our safety, our protection, our refuge, our stronghold because the Lord has promised us: ". . . behold, I am with you always, to the end of the age" [Matthew 28:20b, ESV]. And Hebrews 13: ". . . for He Himself has said, 'I will never leave you nor forsake you.' So we may boldly say: 'The Lord is my helper; I will not fear. What can man do to me?'" [vss.5,6, NKJV].

As a fruit of the spirit, "joy" is an inner effervescence, a delight in the presence of the Lord. Unlike happiness, it is not simply an emotion that comes and goes with circumstances. Joy is a gladness grounded in the truth of what our God has done for us and also promises us for the future: "These things I have spoken to you, that My joy may remain in you, and that your joy may be full" [John 15:11, NKJV].

The joy of the Lord gives us great encouragement, just as it did Jesus in His most desperate hour: ". . . who for the joy that was set before Him endured the cross, despising the shame, and has sat down at the right hand of the throne of God" [Hebrews 12:2, NKJV].

"Finally, my brethren, rejoice [*chairo*-"rejoice exceedingly"] in the Lord," Paul writes to the Philippians" [3:1], and "Rejoice always" [1 Thessalonians 5:16]. Thus we can have joy in the Lord even when unhappy things happen to us: "Count it all joy when you fall into various trials, knowing that the testing of your faith produces patience" [James 1:2,3, ESV].

Those who "abide" in the Lord and continue in His word understand the heart of the prophet Jeremiah who said: "Your words were found, and I did eat them; and your word was unto me the joy and rejoicing of my heart; for I am called by your name, O Lord God of Hosts" [Jeremiah 15:16, NKJV].

Peace

"Peace I leave with you, My peace I give to you; not as the world gives do I give to you. Let not your heart be troubled, neither let it be afraid" [John 14:27, NKJV]. Peace, as a result of walking by the spirit, is the tranquil state of one's soul assured of salvation in Christ and that the Lord God is "our help and our shield" [Psalm 33:20b, NKJV]. The Greek word is *eirene* and means "quietness, tranquility."

Christians have "peace with God through our Lord Jesus Christ," having been "justified [*dikaioo*-"made righteous"] by faith" [Romans 5:1, NKJV]. Therefore, God says, ". . . do not be anxious about anything, but in everything by prayer and supplication, with thanksgiving, let your requests be made known to God. And the peace of God, which surpasses all understanding, will guard your hearts and your minds in Christ Jesus" [Philippians 4:6,7, ESV].

Paul says "let the peace of God rule in your hearts, to which indeed you were called in one body, and be thankful" [Colossians 3:15, ESV]. And Peter writes to believers: "Grace and peace be multiplied to you in the knowledge of God and of Jesus our Lord, as His divine power has given to us all things that pertain to life and godliness, through the knowledge of Him who called us by glory and virtue" [2 Peter 1:2,3, NKJV]. And Jesus says: "These things I have spoken to you, that in Me you may have peace. In the world you will have tribulation, but be of good cheer, I have overcome the world" [John 16:33, NKJV].

Longsuffering (Patience)

Longsuffering [*makrothumia*-"endurance, steadfastness"] is a fruit of the spirit which enables a believer to be especially patient with people before becoming angry. It is the ability to persevere patiently in bearing the offenses, sins, or stubbornness of others and, in the situation of a Christian leader, to be slow to anger, slow to reprimand. It is self-restraint with people in contrast to the biblical use of "patience" [*hupomone*] which is patience with things, not with people.

Paul writes to the Colossians: "May you be strengthened with all power, according to his glorious might, for all endurance [*makrothumia*-"longsuffering"] and patience [*hupomone*] with joy" [Colossians 1:11, ESV]. And he writes to Timothy: "Therefore I endure [*makrothumia*] everything for the sake of the elect, that they also may obtain the salvation that is in Christ Jesus with eternal glory" [2 Timothy 2:10, ESV]. James writes: "As an example of suffering and patience [*makrothumia*], brothers, take the prophets who spoke in the name of the Lord. Behold, we consider those blessed who remained steadfast [*hupomone*]. You have heard of the steadfastness [*hupomone*] of Job, and you have seen the purpose of the Lord, how the Lord is compassionate and merciful" [James 5:10,11, ESV].

Kindness

Jesus said: "Come to me, all who labor and are heavy laden, and I will give you rest. Take my yoke upon you, and learn from me, for I am gentle and lowly in heart, and you will find rest to your souls. For my yoke is easy and my burden is light" [Matthew 11:28-30, ESV]. In the Greek text the word for "easy" is *chrestotes,* meaning "kind." It does not mean "easy." Anyone in longtime Christian service can testify to the reality that the Lord's "yoke" is not "easy," although it is most definitely easier than the lives of most unbelievers. The yoke of the Lord is not always easy, but He is kind.

Kindness, as a fruit of the spirit, seeks the welfare and happiness of others. A believer exhibiting kindness is gracious, mellow, warm-hearted, with an inner disposition to benefit others. Kindness is differentiated from sentimentality and the caretaking of others. Genuine kindness is a strength, not a weakness. Paul says to the Colossians: "Put on, then, as God's chosen ones, holy and beloved, compassionate hearts, kindness, humility, meekness and patience..." [Colossians 3:12, ESV]. To the Ephesians he says: "Be kind to one another, tenderhearted, forgiving one another, as God in Christ forgave you" [Ephesians 4:32]. And to the Corinthians he says: "Love is patient and kind ..." [1 Corinthians 13:4, ESV].

Goodness

"The good person out of the good treasure of his heart produces good," Jesus says in Luke 6:45, "and the evil person out of his evil treasure produces evil, for out of the abundance of his heart his mouth speaks" [ESV]. In the Greek text the word for "good" is *agathos,* and the word for goodness is *agathosune.* They mean "honorable, agreeable, excellent, upright." Goodness, as a fruit of the spirit, upholds standards of moral excellence. It has much in common with kindness, yet "good" and "goodness" in the Bible are contrasted with evil, as in Luke 6:45. For example, it is good of God to punish the evil person, but it's not so good for the one punished.

Paul says to the Romans: "I myself am satisfied about you, my brothers, that you yourselves are full of goodness, filled with all knowledge, and able to instruct one another" [Romans 15:14, ESV]. The NKJV reads: "able to admonish [*noutheteo-* "warn, exhort"] one another." "Goodness" upholds godly standards such as when a Christian shepherd holds his flock accountable for the biblical standards they have been taught. "Longsuffering" and "kindness" may enable the leader to bear with their spiritual immaturity, but not to the fault of failing to admonish, warn or exhort when necessary. Paul says to the Romans: ". . . we know that the judgment of God is according to truth . . . Or do you despise the riches of His goodness, forbearance, and longsuffering, not knowing that the goodness [moral excellence, integrity] of God leads you to repentance?" [Romans 2:2a,4, NKJV].

Faithfulness

Faithfulness [*pistos*] is a steadfast trust in and adherence to our Heavenly Father's word and will. While many people may believe in, that is, have faith in some things of God when it is convenient, "faithfulness," as a fruit of the spirit, is a persevering trust in God's promises day in and day out, despite circumstances.

"Forever, O Lord, your word is settled in heaven. Your faithfulness endures to all generations" [Psalm 119:90, NKJV]. "Through the Lord's mercies we are not consumed because His compassions fail not. They are new every morning; great is your faithfulness" [Lamentations 3:22,23, NKJV]. Paul says to the Corinthians: "Let a man so consider us, as servants of Christ and stewards of the mysteries of God. Moreover it is required in stewards that one be found faithful" [*pistos*-"worthy of trust"] [1 Corinthians 4:1,2, NKJV].

Meekness (Gentleness)

Meekness [*praytes*-"humility, gentleness, submissiveness"] is a humble, submissive attitude toward the will of God. Jesus said: "Take My yoke upon you and learn of Me, for I am meek [*praos*-"gentle"] and lowly in heart, and you shall find rest unto your souls" [Matthew 11:29, NKJV]. Biblically, "meekness" is the ability to be humble and submissive toward God and spiritual authority, to be teachable and coachable without becoming upset or tempted to seek revenge. "Now the man Moses was very humble [*anav*-"meek"], more than all men who were on the face of the earth" [Numbers 12:3, NKJV].

"Meekness" is a spiritual strength rather than a weakness such as being "wimpy" or cowardly, and it is the opposite of being demanding or arrogant. Paul asks the Corinthians: "What do you want? Shall I come to you with a rod, or in love and a spirit of gentleness?" [*praotes*—"meekness"] [1 Corinthians 4:21, NKJV]. James says: "Who is wise and understanding among you? Let him show by good conduct that his works are done in the meekness [*praytes*-"gentleness of spirit"] of wisdom" [James 3:13, NKJV].

Self-control

"Self-control," as a fruit of the spirit, is the ability to master one's passions and desires. The word of God is the high standard by which our Heavenly Father wants His children to practice self-control [*egkrateia*-"the virtue of one who master's himself"]. He does not leave us without recourse but, being loving, very compassionate and merciful [James 5:11b], He provides us with the ability to control our human desires and passions by means of the gift of holy spirit working in us and the ongoing renewal of our minds to His word. "No temptation has overtaken you except such as is common to man," Paul writes to the Corinthians, "but God is faithful, who will not allow you to be tempted beyond what you are able, but with the temptation will also make the way of escape that you may be able to bear it" [1 Corinthians 10:13, NKJV].

"Therefore, beloved," he says, "flee from idolatry" [*eidololatria*-"vices springing from rebellion against God"] [v. 14]. To the Colossians Paul says: "Put to death therefore what is earthly in you: sexual immorality, impurity, passion, evil desire, and covetousness, which is idolatry" [Colossians 3:5, ESV].

God's word sets a high standard for us. The standard of the world is "whatever feels good, do it." But self-control, as a fruit of the spirit, is mastering—situation by situation—our fleshly desires. It is not merely attempting to overcome sinful temptations by means of outward religious practices, as if our old nature could be "reformed" so as to mitigate those desires. True self-control is not entirely dependent on our will power; rather it is a spiritual virtue resulting from our systematic progress in "the Lord's curriculum."

Asyndenton

The "fruit of the spirit" listed in Galatians 5:22,23 is not an exhaustive list; rather, in its totality it is a figure of speech—*asyndeton*—which is a stylistic presentation in which conjunctions are omitted to make a singular point. The singular point of the "fruit of the spirit" taken together is a presentation of "the character of Christ" to be formed in God's people. "Against such there is no law" [Galatians 5:23, NKJV]. "And those who are Christ's have crucified the flesh with its passions and desires," Paul continues. "If we live in the Spirit, let us also walk in the Spirit" [vss. 24,25]. Paul makes this point emphatically when he declares: "I have been crucified with Christ. It is no longer I who live, but Christ who lives in me. And the life I now live in the flesh I live by faith in the Son of God, who loved me and gave himself for me" [Galatians 2:20, ESV].

Summary
"The fruit of the Spirit"

The Lord wants the members of His Body to "bear fruit with patience." He has given us guidelines by which we may ascertain our progress.

Verse to Remember: "But the fruit of the spirit is love, joy, peace, patience, kindness, goodness, faithfulness, gentleness, self-control; against such things there is no law" [Galatians 5:22,23, ESV].

Questions to ask Myself: How am I doing, Lord? What "fruit of the spirit" do I need to improve on?

Exercise: Choose a "fruit of the spirit" you want to have ripen more beautifully in your life. Determine how you can work on this, and do it.

TEN

How did He do it?

How did Jesus do it? How did He heal the sick, open the eyes of the blind, and set the captives free at every opportunity? And how did His apostles and disciples do it after He left this earth and ascended into heaven to be with His Father? Some may say: "Jesus could do it because He was God," suggesting that we cannot because we are not God. But that explanation is born of blind faith. Yet over and over in his letters to the Church, Paul writes: "I would not have you ignorant" or "I do not want you to be uninformed" regarding spiritual matters. In 1 Corinthians 2 he says: "Yet among the [spiritually] mature we do impart wisdom, although it is not a wisdom of this age or of the rulers of this age, who are doomed to pass away. But we impart a secret and hidden wisdom of God, which God decreed before the ages for our glory. None of the rulers of this age understood this, for if they had, they would not have crucified the Lord of glory. But, as it is written, 'What no eye has seen, nor ear heard, nor the heart of man imagined, what God has prepared for those who love him'—these things God has revealed to us through the Spirit. For the Spirit searches everything, even the depths of God. For who knows a person's thoughts except the spirit of that person, which is in him? So also no one comprehends the thoughts of God except the Spirit of God. Now we have received not the spirit of the world, but the Spirit who is from God, that we might understand the things freely given us by God. And we impart this in words not taught by human wisdom but taught by the Spirit, interpreting spiritual truths to those who are spiritual" [vss. 6-13, ESV].

As we have seen in previous chapters in this study, the word of God reveals keys to help us understand how Jesus did it and how His disciples can do it today. In John 5:30 Jesus says: "I can do nothing on my own. As I hear, I judge, and my judgment is just, because I seek not my own will but the will of him who sent me" [ESV]. This is an important truth for followers of Christ to understand. In John 6:38 He says: "For I have come down from heaven, not to do my own will but the will of him who sent me" [ESV]. In John 7:17 He says: "My teaching is not mine, but his who sent me" [ESV]. And in John 8:26 He says: "I have much to say about you and much to judge, but he who sent me is true, and I declare to the world what I have heard from him" [ESV].

Luke 4:1,2 informs us that "Jesus, full of Holy Spirit, returned from the Jordan [where "Jesus also had been baptized and was praying, the heavens were opened, and the Holy Spirit descended on him in bodily form, like a dove"—John 3:22, ESV] and was led by the Spirit in the wilderness for forty days, being tempted by the devil" [ESV]. What was Jesus doing in the wilderness for forty days? He was learning to "walk by the spirit"—learning to listen to the "still small voice" of His Father via the spirit that had descended on Him. That is to say, He was learning to operate the "manifestations of the spirit" [see chapter 5]—spiritual revelation from His Father: "the word of knowledge"—information from God via the spirit on Him which He could not know by His senses; "the word of wisdom"—*what to do* about the information received; "prophecy"—inspired utterance from God via the spirit in accordance with the word of God which He had meticulously studied all of His life—"*It is written . . . ;*" "the discerning of spirits"—revelation regarding the presence or non-presence of demon spirits and whether or not He should cast them out; "believing faith"—absolute conviction that as He followed through on what His Father was revealing to Him via a word of knowledge and a word of wisdom and/or the discerning of spirits, that healing or another miracle would take place; the "working of miracles" and "gifts of healing"—the demonstration of the love and mercy and power of God via spiritual energy to bring about the miraculous, whether to "turn water into wine" or to effect deliverance from demonic oppressions or to impart a gift of healing—a true gift of God's love.

This is how Jesus did it. During His ministry on earth, Jesus operated seven of the nine manifestations of the spirit Paul spells out in 1 Corinthians 12. Jesus did not speak in tongues nor did He interpret tongues because these are manifestations of the spirit specifically for the members of His spiritual Body made available for the first time on the Day of Pentecost. Jesus did not need to "edify" His spirit daily, as the members of His Body must do, because He had the "fullness of God" [Colossians 1:19] from the onset of His baptism.

Jesus said: *"I can do nothing on my own; as I hear I judge"* [italics supplied]. Everything He did He did in accordance with His Father's instructions and direction by means of the spirit upon Him. And every example of healing and deliverance recorded in the four Gospels which Jesus did is a *teachable lesson.* "He who has ears to hear, let him hear!" [Matthew 11:15,NKJV].

Water into wine (John 2)

"This, the first of his signs, Jesus did at Cana of Galilee, and manifested his glory. And his disciples believed in him" [John 2:11, ESV]. Jesus and His disciples were invited to a wedding feast at Cana in Galilee, and when the wine ran out, Jesus turned water into wine. How did He do it? The Scriptures say: "Now there were six stone water jars for the Jewish rites of purification, each holding twenty or thirty gallons. Jesus said to the servants, 'Fill the jars with water.' And they filled them up to the brim. And he said to them, 'Now draw some out and take it to the master of the feast.' So they took it. When the master of the feast tasted the water now become wine, and did not know where it came from (though the servants who had drawn the water knew), the master of the feast called the bridegroom and said to him, 'Everyone serves the good wine first, and when people have drunk freely, then the poor wine. But you have kept the good wine until now'" [vss. 6-10, ESV]. Intending to manifest His Son's glory to His disciples and bring attention to His ministry, God revealed to Jesus exactly how He should handle the situation. By means of "the manifestation of the word of knowledge," God gave Jesus, via the spirit upon Him, specific information regarding the situation which He could not know by His senses. At the same time, by means of "the manifestation of the word of wisdom," God told His Son exactly *what to do* with the information in order to bring to pass a miracle—turning the water into wine. As Jesus acted in absolute conviction (via the manifestation of believing faith)— "Fill the jar with water . . . now draw some out and take it to the master of the feast"—the miracle came to pass as God intended. Jesus was simply "walking by the spirit," listening to the "still small voice" of His Father guiding Him by means of the spirit upon Him. It's important for us to understand God's purpose in guiding His Son to turn the water into wine. It was not Jesus' own determination or will to glorify Himself. "I can do nothing on my own; as I hear I judge." And: "I seek not my own will, but the will of him who sent me."

At the conclusion of his gospel, John informs us that "there are also many other things that Jesus did, which if they were written one by one, I suppose that even the world itself could not contain the books that would be written" [John 21:25, NKJV]. In this chapter we present a few examples from each of the four Gospels illustrating how Jesus "walked by the spirit" in order to "heal the brokenhearted, to proclaim liberty to the captives, and recovery of sight to the blind, to set at liberty those who are oppressed, to proclaim the acceptable year of the Lord" [Luke 4:18b, 19, NKJV].

The centurion's servant (Matthew 8)

"Now when Jesus had entered Capernaum, a centurion came to Him, pleading with Him, saying, 'Lord, my servant is lying at home paralyzed dreadfully tormented.' And Jesus said to him, 'I will come and heal him.' The centurion answered and said, 'Lord, I am not worthy that you should come under my roof. But only speak a word, and my servant will be healed. For I also am a man under authority, having soldiers under me. And I say to this one, 'Go,' and he goes; and to another, 'Come,' and he comes; and to my servant, 'Do this,' and he does it.' When Jesus heard it, He marveled, and said to those who followed, 'Assuredly, I say to you, I have not found such great faith, not even in Israel . . . And Jesus said to the centurion, 'Go your way; and as you have believed, so let it be done for you'" [Matthew 8:5-10,13, NKJV]. We notice here the centurion's great faith in Jesus and in His word. He understood that Jesus was "under authority," just as he himself was and that His word must be obeyed. Herein is an example of "faith meeting faith" in a spiritual continuum. The centurion had absolute faith that Jesus could heal his servant, even at a distance. And Jesus had absolute faith that it was His Father's will for the servant to receive healing. Walking by the spirit, Jesus said, "I will come and heal him," having received from the Father via the spirit upon Him the necessary "word of knowledge"—information regarding the situation and the man's great faith—and "word of wisdom"—precisely *what to do* with the information received. "Go your way," He said to the centurion, "and as you have believed, so let it be done for you." Immediately the centurion's servant was healed which, indeed, was the manifestation of a miracle and the manifestation of a gift of healing.

"Arise, take up your bed" (Matthew 9)

"Then, behold, they brought to him a paralytic lying on a bed. When Jesus saw their faith [faith meeting faith], He said to the paralytic, 'Son, be of good cheer, your sins are forgiven you' [word of knowledge from the Father]. "And at once some of the scribes said within themselves, 'This man blasphemes!' But Jesus, knowing their thoughts, said, 'Why do you think evil in your hearts? For which is easier, to say, 'Your sins are forgiven you,' or to say, 'Arise and walk?' But that you may know that the Son of Man has power [*exousia*-"exercised authority, permission"] on earth to forgive sins—then He said to the paralytic, 'Arise, take up your bed, and go to your house' [word of wisdom, manifestation of believing faith]. And he arose [miracle and gift of healing] and departed to his house" [Matthew 9:2-7, NKJV]. Faith is simple trust. It's clear in this record that all those who brought the paralyzed man to Jesus had faith in His ability to heal. Despite the intense unbelief from the "religious establishment"—the scribes—in the crowd, Jesus responded to the faith of the few.

"Beware of false prophets" (Matthew 7)

"Beware of false prophets, who come to you in sheep's clothing, but inwardly they are ravenous wolves. You will know them by their fruits . . . Not everyone who says to me, 'Lord, Lord,' shall enter the kingdom of heaven, but he who does the will of My Father in heaven. Many will say to me in that day, 'Lord, Lord, have we not prophesied in Your name, cast out demons in Your name, and done many wonders in Your name?' And then I will declare to them, 'I never knew you; depart from Me, you who practice lawlessness!'" [word of knowledge, word of wisdom, manifestation of prophecy of a prophet] [Matthew 7:15, 16a, 21-23, NKJV]. Little has changed in more than two thousand years. Many false prophets operate in the Church today. They prophesy in the name of Jesus, they cast out demons in His name, they do wonders in His name. But behind the scenes, they are in it for the money and the personal fame. Jesus will declare to them: "I never knew you; depart from Me, you who practice lawlessness!"

"a withered hand" (Matthew 12)

"Now when He had departed from there, He went into their synagogue. And behold, there was a man who had a withered hand. And they asked Him, saying, 'Is it lawful to heal on the Sabbath?'—that they might accuse Him. Then He said to them, 'What man is there among you who has one sheep, and if it falls into a pit on the Sabbath, will not lay hold of it and lift it out? Of how much more value then is a man than a sheep? Therefore it is lawful to do good on the Sabbath.' Then He said to the man, 'Stretch out your hand' [word of knowledge, word of wisdom, believing faith]. And he stretched it out [miracle], and it was restored as whole as the other" [gift of healing] [Matthew 12:10-13, NKJV]. This record is similar to those in Mark 3:1-5 and Luke 6:6-11. It does not say that the man with the withered hand had faith to be healed. However, it is clear that the man obeyed Jesus when He told him to stretch out his hand. In many Gospel records of healing and deliverance, both the individual and the Lord had faith—faith meeting faith. However, in some instances only the Lord, walking in faith at all times, operated the manifestation of believing faith according to the message of knowledge and message of wisdom received from His Father. Another such instance is the healing of the high priest's ear which Peter had cut off with the sword (Luke 22:51). This tells us that it is not always necessary for *both* the minister and the person being ministered to to have faith for healing or for another working of miracles.

"walking on the water" (Matthew 14)

"Immediately Jesus made His disciples get into the boat and go before Him to the other side, while He sent the multitudes away. And when He had sent the multitudes away, He went up on the mountain by Himself to pray. Now when evening came, He was alone there. But the boat was now in the middle of the sea, tossed by the waves, for the wind was contrary. Now in the fourth watch of the night Jesus went to them, walking on the sea [word of knowledge, word of wisdom, believing faith, miracle]. And when the disciples saw Him walking on the sea, they were troubled, saying, 'It is a ghost!' And they cried out for fear. But immediately Jesus spoke to them, saying, 'Be of good cheer! It is I; do not be afraid.' And Peter answered Him, and said, 'Lord, if it is You, command me to come to You on the water.' So He said, 'Come' [word of knowledge, word of wisdom]. And when Peter had come down out of the boat, he walked on the water to go to Jesus [believing faith, miracle]. But when he saw that the wind was boisterous, he was afraid, and beginning to sink, he cried out, saying, 'Lord, save me!' And immediately Jesus stretched out His hand and caught him, and said to him, 'O you of little faith, why did you doubt?'" [word of knowledge, word of wisdom, believing faith, miracle] [Matthew 14:22-31, ESV]. Peter was able to walk on water for a moment because in faith he mustered the courage to step "out of his comfort zone." Anyone stepping forward to be ministered to for healing or other deliverance—or to speak in tongues for the first time or prophesy for the first time in a fellowship—must absolutely step "out of his comfort zone" and obey the word of God.

Feeding the four thousand (Matthew 15)

"Now Jesus called His disciples to Himself and said, 'I have compassion on the multitude because they have continued with me three days and have nothing to eat. And I do not want to send them away hungry, lest they faint on the way.' Then His disciples said to Him, 'Where could we get enough bread in the wilderness to fill such a multitude?' Jesus said to them, 'How many loaves do you have?' And they said, 'Seven, and a few little fish.' So He commanded the multitude to sit down on the ground. And He took the seven loaves and the fish and gave thanks, broke them and gave them to His disciples [word of knowledge, word of wisdom, believing faith]; and the disciples gave to the multitude. So they all ate and were filled [miracles], and they took up seven large baskets that were left. Now those who ate were four thousand men, besides women and children" [Matthew 15:32-38].

The feeding of the "four thousand men, besides women and children," recorded in this chapter, as well as the five thousand recorded in John 9, is an example of God's phenomenal benevolence and provision for His people. Jesus said "I can do nothing on my own; as I hear [from the Father] I judge, and my judgment is just because I seek not my own will but the will of him who sent me" [John 5:30, ESV]. God gives His Son the knowledge of what is to be done and the instruction [wisdom] in exactly how to accomplish it and Jesus, acting in obedience and believing faith [absolute conviction], works the miracles by means of the power [*dunamis*] in Him.

"He was transfigured before them" (Matthew 17)

"Now after six days Jesus took Peter, James, and John his brother, led them up on a high mountain by themselves; and He was transfigured [*metamorphoo*-"changed into another form"] before them. His face shone like the sun, and His clothes became as white as the light [a phenomenon—the special grace of God]. And behold, Moses and Elijah appeared to them, talking with Him [word of knowledge, believing faith, miracle]. Then Peter answered and said to Jesus, 'Lord, it is good for us to be here; if You wish, let us make here three tabernacles: one for You, one for Moses, and one for Elijah.' While he was still speaking, behold, a bright cloud overshadowed them; and suddenly a voice came out of the cloud, saying, 'This is My beloved Son, in whom I am well pleased. Hear Him!' [phenomenon]. And when the disciples heard it, they fell on their faces and were greatly afraid. But Jesus came and touched them and said, 'Arise, and do not be afraid.' When they had lifted up their eyes, they saw no one but Jesus only. Now as they came down from the mountain, Jesus commanded them, saying, 'Tell the vision to no one until the Son of Man is risen from the dead' [word of knowledge, word of wisdom]. And His disciples asked Him, saying, 'Why then do the scribes say that Elijah must come first?' Jesus answered and said to them, 'Indeed, Elijah is coming first and will restore all things. But I say to you that Elijah has come already, and they did not know him but did to him whatever they wished. Likewise the Son of Man is about to suffer at their hands' [word of knowledge, word of wisdom]. Then the disciples understood that He spoke to them of John the Baptist" [Matthew 17:1-13, NKJV].

"Take, eat; this is My body" (Matthew 26)

"When evening had come, He sat down with the twelve. Now as they were eating, He said, 'Assuredly, I say to you, one of you will betray Me' [word of knowledge, word of wisdom]. And they were exceedingly sorrowful, and each of them began to say to Him, 'Lord, is it I?' He answered and said, 'He who dipped his hand with Me in the dish will betray Me. The Son of Man goes just as it is written of Him, but woe to that man by whom the Son of Man is betrayed! It would have been good for that man if he had not been born.' Then Judas, who was betraying Him, answered and said, 'Rabbi, is it I?' He said to him, 'You have said it.' And as they were eating, Jesus took bread [*artos*—ordinary table bread. Clearly this was not the Passover meal for if it had been, the Law would have required that unleavened bread—*azymos*—be used.], blessed and broke it, and gave it to the disciples [word of knowledge, word of wisdom] and said, 'Take, eat; this is My body' [prophecy]. Then He took the cup, and gave thanks and gave it to them, saying, 'Drink from it, all of you. For this is My blood of the new covenant, which is shed for many for the remission of sins. But I say to you, I will not drink of this fruit of the vine from now on until that day when I drink it new with you in My Father's kingdom'" [word of knowledge, word of wisdom, prophecy] [Matthew 26:20-29,NKJV].

"Who touched Me?" (Mark 5)

"Now a certain woman had a flow of blood for twelve years, and had suffered many things from many physicians. She had spent all that she had and was no better, but grew worse. When she heard about Jesus, she came behind Him in the crowd and touched His garment. For she said, 'If only I may touch His clothes, I shall be made well.' Immediately the fountain of her blood was dried up [miracle, gift of healing] and she felt in her body that she was healed of the affliction. And Jesus, immediately knowing in Himself that power [*dunamis*-"inherent power, some texts read "virtue"] had gone out of Him [word of knowledge, word of wisdom], turned around in the crowd and said, 'Who touched My clothes?' But His disciples said to Him, 'You see the multitude thronging You, and You say, 'Who touched Me?' And He looked around to see her who had done this thing. But the woman, fearing and trembling, knowing what had happened to her, came and fell down before Him and told Him the whole truth. And He said to her, 'Daughter, your faith [faith touching faith] has made you whole. Go in peace, and be healed of your affliction'" [Mark 5:25-34, NKJV]. "And Jesus, immediately knowing in Himself that power had gone out of Him . . . ." Jesus had the power [*dumanis*] and the authority [*exousia*] to exercise that power. Where did He get it? His Father gave it to Him when He was baptized with the spirit. All He needed from His Father in this situation, and in every situation of healing and deliverance recorded in the Gospels, was guidance from His Father to proceed.

"Little girl, I say to you, arise" (Mark 5)

"While He was still speaking, some came from the ruler of the synagogue's house who said, 'Your daughter is dead. Why trouble the Teacher any further?' As soon as Jesus heard the word that was spoken, He said to the ruler of the synagogue, 'Do not be afraid; only believe.' And He permitted no one to follow them except Peter, James, and John the brother of James [word of knowledge, word of wisdom]. Then He came to the house of the ruler of the synagogue, and saw a tumult and those who wept and wailed loudly. When He came in, He said to them, 'Why make this commotion and weep? The child is not dead, but sleeping' [word of knowledge]. And they ridiculed Him. But when He had put them all outside [word of wisdom], He took the father and the mother of the child, and those who were with Him, and entered where the child was lying. Then He took the child by the hand [word of knowledge, word of wisdom, believing faith], and said to her, 'Talitha, cumi,' which is translated, 'Little girl, I say to you, arise.' Immediately the girl arose [miracle] and walked [gift of healing], for she was twelve years of age. And they were overcome with great amazement" [Mark 5:35-42, NKJV].

In this situation, Jesus "permitted no one to follow them except Peter, James, and John" because of the people's unbelief. Likewise, He took the father and mother of the child, and those who were with Him, and entered where the child was lying" because of their expectation in faith. Jesus was simply walking by the spirit.

"My name is Legion" (Mark 5)

"Then they came to the other side of the sea, to the country of the Gadarenes. And when He had come out of the boat, immediately there met Him out of the tombs a man with an unclean spirit, who had his dwelling among the tombs; and no one could bind him, not even with chains, because he had often been bound with shackles and chains. And the chains had been pulled apart by him, and the shackles broken in pieces; neither could anyone tame him. And always, night and day, he was in the mountains and in the tombs, crying out and cutting himself with stones. When he saw Jesus from afar, he ran and worshipped Him. And he [a demon] cried out with a loud voice and said, 'What have I to do with you, Jesus, Son of the Most High God? I implore you by God that You do not torment me.' [Demons know Jesus and that there is a time coming when they will be bound and destroyed—Daniel 7:12; Revelation 20:10]. For He said to him [Jesus spoke to the demon, not to the man], 'Come out of the man, unclean spirit!' [word of knowledge, word of wisdom, discerning of spirits, believing faith]. Then He asked him [the demon], 'What is your name?' And he answered, 'My name is Legion; for we are many.' Also he begged Him earnestly that He would not send them out of the country. Now a large heard of swine was feeding there near the mountains. So all the demons begged Him, saying, 'Send us to the swine, that we may enter them.' And at once Jesus gave them permission. Then the unclean spirits went out and entered the swine [miracle] (there were about two thousand); and the herd ran violently down the steep place into the sea, and drowned in the sea. So those who fed the swine fled, and they told it in the city and in the country. And they went out to see what it was that had happened. Then they came to Jesus, and saw the one who had been demon-possessed and had the legion, sitting and clothed and in his right mind [gift of healing]. And they were afraid" [Mark 5:1-15, NKJV].

"And He marveled because of their unbelief" (Mark 6)

"Then He went out from there and came to His country, and His disciples followed Him. And when the Sabbath had come He began to teach in the synagogue. And many hearing Him were astonished, saying, 'Where did this man get these things? And what wisdom is this which is given to Him, that such mighty works are performed by His hands? Is this not the carpenter, the son of Mary, and brother of James, Joses, Judas, and Simon? And are not His sisters here with us?' So they were offended at Him. But Jesus said to them, 'A prophet is not without honor except in his own country, among his own relatives, and in his own house.' Now He could do no mighty work there except that He laid His hands on a few sick people and healed them [word of knowledge, word of wisdom, believing faith, miracles, gifts of healing]. And He marveled because of their unbelief." [Mark 6:1-6,NKJV.

Herein is a spiritual principle: Unbelief *defeats* the promises of God. Believing faith *appropriates* the promises of God. Even the Son of God "could do no mighty work there" because of the people's unbelief.

"one who was deaf" (Mark 7)

"Then they brought to Him one who was deaf and had an impediment in his speech, and they begged Him to put His hand on him. And He took him aside from the multitude [word of knowledge] and put His fingers in his ears [word of wisdom], and He spat and touched his tongue [word of wisdom, believing faith]. Then, looking up to heaven [thanking His Father], He sighed, and said to him, 'Ephphata,' that is, 'Be opened' [word of wisdom, believing faith]. Immediately his ears were opened, and the impediment of his tongue was loosed [miracles, gifts of healing], and he spoke plainly. Then He commanded them that they should tell no one; but the more He commanded them, the more widely they proclaimed it. And they were astonished beyond measure, saying, 'He has done all things well. He makes both the deaf to hear and the mute to speak'" [Mark 7:32- 37, NKJV].

"a blind man" (Mark 8)

"Then He came to Bethsaida; and they brought a blind man to Him, and begged Him to touch him. So He took the blind man by the hand and led him out of the town [word of knowledge, word of wisdom]. And when He had spit on his eyes and put His hands on him [word of knowledge, word of wisdom, believing faith], He asked him if he saw anything. And he looked up and said, 'I see men like trees, walking.' Then He put His hands on his eyes again [word of knowledge, word of wisdom] and made him look up. And he was restored and saw everything clearly" [miracle, gift of healing] [Mark 8:22-25, NKJV].

"If you can believe, all things are possible" (Mark 9)

"And when He came to the disciples, He saw a great multitude around them. Immediately, when they saw Him, all the people were greatly amazed, and running to Him, greeted Him. And He asked the scribes, 'What are you discussing with them?' Then one of the crowd answered and said, 'Teacher, I brought You my son, who has a mute spirit. And whenever it seizes him, it throws him down; he foams at the mouth, gnashes his teeth, and becomes rigid. So I spoke to your disciples, that they should cast it out, but they could not.' He answered him, and said, 'O faithless generation, how long shall I be with you? How long shall I bear with you? Bring him to me.' Then they brought him to Him. And when he saw him, immediately the [demon] spirit convulsed him, and he fell on the ground and wallowed, foaming at the mouth. So He asked his father, 'How long has this been happening to him?' And he said, 'From childhood. And often he [it] has thrown him both into the fire and into the water to destroy him. But if You can do anything, have compassion on us and help us.' Jesus said to him, 'If you can believe, all things are possible to him who believes.' Immediately the father of the child cried out and said with tears, 'Lord, I believe; help my unbelief.'"

Herein is an important truth believers need to understand. Despite His reputation as a healer and the signs, miracles, and wonders that authenticated His ministry, still Jesus had to deal with pervasive unbelief among the people. And it is a sobering reality that for many mature Christians today, even though we "have tasted that the Lord is gracious" [1 Peter 2:3] all our lives, still we have unbelief in our "old self" that says "seeing is believing" instead of our "new self"— the Christ in you—that says "believe—and then you will see." That's why we must "abide in Him" by persisting in "the Lord's curriculum," especially praying perseveringly for His help.

"When Jesus saw that the people came running together, He rebuked the unclean spirit, saying to it: 'Deaf and dumb spirit, I command you, come out of him and enter him no more!' [word of knowledge, word of wisdom, discerning of spirits, believing faith]. Then the spirit cried out, convulsed him greatly, and came out of him [miracle]. And he [the child] became as one dead, so that many said, 'He is dead.' But Jesus took him by the hand and lifted him up, and he arose [word of knowledge, word of wisdom, believing faith, gift of healing]. And when He had come into the house, His disciples asked Him privately, 'Why could we not cast it out?' So He said to them, 'This kind [of demon spirit] can come out by nothing but prayer and fasting'" [strong faith as the result of one's prayer life, renewal of the mind, and doing the will of God] [Mark 9:14-29,NKJV].

"I am willing; be cleansed" (Luke 5)

"And it happened that when He was in a certain city, that behold, a man who was full of leprosy saw Jesus; and he fell on his face and implored Him, saying, 'Lord, if You are willing, You can make me clean.' Then He put out His hand and touched him, saying, 'I am willing; be cleansed' [word of knowledge, word of wisdom, believing faith]. Immediately the leprosy left him [miracle, gift of healing]. And He charged him to tell no one, 'But go and show yourself to the priest, and make an offering for your cleansing, as a testimony to them, just as Moses commanded'" [Luke 5:12-14, NKJV]. Jesus was willing. He is willing today.

"He healed them all" (Luke 6)

"And He came down with them and stood on a level place with a crowd of His disciples and a great multitude of people from all Judea and Jerusalem, and from the seacoast of Tyre and Sidon, who came to hear Him and be healed of their diseases, as well as those who were tormented with unclean spirits. And they were healed [word of knowledge, word of wisdom, discerning of spirits, believing faith, miracles, gifts of healing]. And the whole multitude sought to touch Him, for power [*dunamis*] went out from Him and healed them all" [Luke 6:17-19, NKJV].

"Mary called Magdalene" (Luke 8)

"And it came to pass, afterwards, that He went through every city and village, preaching and bringing the glad tidings of the kingdom of God. And the twelve were with Him, and certain women who had been healed of evil spirits and infirmities [word of knowledge, word of wisdom, discerning of spirits, believing faith, miracles, gifts of healing]—Mary called Magdalene, out of whom had come seven demons, and Joanna the wife of Chuza, Herod's steward, and Susanna, and many others who provided for Him from their substance" [Luke 8:1-3, NKJV]. No doubt Mary had to persist in difficult and challenging lifestyle changes in order to keep the demons out. In doing so she became a devout follower of Jesus, and she was the first person to witness His resurrection out from among the dead (John 20).

The twelve sent forth (Luke 9)

"Then He called His twelve disciples together and gave them power [*dunamis*-"inherent ability"] and authority [*exousia*-"permission, liberty"] over all demons and to cure diseases. He sent them to preach the kingdom of God and to heal the sick" [by means of the manifestations of word of knowledge, word of wisdom, discerning of spirits, believing faith, miracles and gifts of healing—revelation from the Father via the spirit upon each of them] [Luke 9:1,2, NKJV]. The apostles were not "born" of the spirit at this time; they had spirit "upon" them temporarily in order to fulfill the specific mission for which the Lord commissioned them.

"a spirit of infirmity" (Luke 13)

"Now He was teaching in one of the synagogues on the Sabbath. And behold, there was a woman who had a spirit of infirmity eighteen years, and was bent over and could in no way raise herself up. But when Jesus saw her, He called her to Him and said to her, 'Woman, you are loosed from your infirmity.' And He laid His hands on her [word of knowledge, word of woman, discerning of spirits] and immediately she was made straight [believing faith, miracle, gift of healing] and glorified God" [Luke 13:10-13, NKJV].

"... are you betraying the Son of Man with a kiss?" (Luke 22)

"And while He was still speaking, behold, a multitude; and he who was called Judas, one of the twelve, went before them and drew near to Jesus to kiss Him. But Jesus said to him, 'Judas, are you betraying the Son of Man with a kiss?' When those around Him saw what was going to happen, they said to Him, 'Lord, shall we strike with the sword?' And one of them struck the servant of the high priest and cut off his right ear. But Jesus answered and said, 'Permit even this.' And He touched his ear and healed him [word of knowledge, word of wisdom, believing faith, miracle, gift of healing] [Luke 22:47-51, NKJV]. God's mercy is amazing, inspiring His Son to reach out and heal the servant's ear. Do you suppose that this man, washing the blood off his head and clothes, touching his ear repeatedly to make sure it was really healed, wondered deeply—"Who is this Jesus?"—throughout the night, even as he witnessed the Lord's torture at the hands of his cohorts?

The road to Emmaus (Luke 24)

"Now behold, two of them were traveling that same day to a village called Emmaus, which was seven miles from Jerusalem. And they talked together of all these things which had happened. So it was, while they conversed and reasoned, that Jesus Himself drew near and went with them [word of knowledge, word of wisdom, believing faith, miracle]. But their eyes were restrained so that they did not know Him. And He said to them, 'What kind of conversation is this that you have with one another as you walk and are sad?' Then the one whose name was Cleopus answered and said to Him, 'Are you the only stranger in Jerusalem, and have you not known the things which happened there in these days?' And He said to them, 'What things?' So they said to Him, 'The things concerning Jesus of Nazareth, who was a Prophet mighty in deed and word before God and all the people, and how the chief priests and our rulers delivered Him to be condemned to death, and crucified Him. But we were hoping that it was He who was going to redeem Israel. Indeed, besides all this, today is the third day since these things happened. Yes, and certain women of our company, who arrived at the tomb early astonished us. They came saying that they had also seen a vision of angels who said He was alive. And certain of those who were with us went to the tomb and found it just as the women had said; but Him they did not see.' Then He said to them, 'O foolish ones, and slow of heart to believe in all that the prophets have spoken! Ought not the Christ to have suffered these things and to enter into His glory?' And beginning at Moses and all the prophets, He expounded to them in all the Scriptures the things concerning Himself [prophecy]. Then they drew near to the village where they were going, and He indicated that He would have gone further. But they constrained Him, saying, 'Abide with us, for it is toward evening, and the day is far spent.' And He went in to stay with them. Now it came to pass, as He sat at the table with them, that He took bread, blessed and broke it, and gave it to them. Then their eyes were opened and they knew Him [miracle]; and He vanished out of their sight [miracle—phenomenon, a super manifestation of the resurrected Christ]. And they said to one another, 'Did not our heart burn within us while He talked with us on the road, and while He opened the Scriptures to us?'" [Luke 24:13-32, NKJV]. "For the word of God is living, and powerful, and sharper than any two-edged sword . . . ." Do not our hearts burn within us when we open the Scriptures and allow them to reveal to us the Living Christ?

"Rise, take up your bed, and walk" (John 5)

"Now there is in Jerusalem by the Sheep Gate a pool, which is called in Hebrew, Bethesda, having five porches. In these lay a great multitude of sick people, blind, lame, paralyzed, waiting for the moving of the water. For an angel went down at a certain time into the pool and stirred up the water; then whoever stepped in first, after the stirring of the water, was made well of whatever disease he had [the preceding verse is omitted from most Greek manuscripts]. Now a certain man was there who had an infirmity thirty-eight years. When Jesus saw him lying there, He said to him, 'Do you want to be made well?' The sick man answered Him, 'I have no man to put me into the pool when the water is stirred up; but while I am coming, another steps down before me.' Jesus said to him, 'Rise, take up your bed, and walk' [word of knowledge, word of wisdom, believing faith]. And immediately the man was made well, took up his bed, and walked [miracle, gift of healing]. And that day was the Sabbath" [John 5:2-9, NKJV]. Here is another example of "faith meeting faith" for a miracle to occur: it's clear that the man with the infirmity had been "waiting for the moving of the water" in complete faith that if he could only get into the pool when the water was stirred, he would be made well.

Feeding the five thousand (John 6)

"Then Jesus lifted up His eyes, and seeing a great multitude coming toward Him, He said to Philip, 'Where shall we buy bread that these may eat?' But this He said to test him, for He Himself knew what He would do [word of knowledge, word of wisdom, believing faith]. Philip answered Him, 'Two hundred denari worth of bread is not sufficient for them, that every one of them may have a little.' One of His disciples, Andrew, Simon Peter's brother, said to Him, 'There is a lad here who has five barley loaves and two small fish, but what are they among so many?' Then Jesus said, 'Make the people sit down.' Now there was much grass in the place. So the men sat down, in number about five thousand. And Jesus took the loaves, and when He had given thanks He distributed them to the disciples, and the disciples to those sitting down; and likewise of the fish, as much as they wanted [a miracle compounded]. So when they were filled, He said to His disciples, 'Gather up the fragments that remain, so that nothing is lost.' Therefore they gathered them up, and filled twelve baskets with the fragments of the five barley loaves which were left over by those who had eaten, Then those men, when they had seen the sign which Jesus did, said, 'This is truly the Prophet who is to come into the world'" [John 6:5-14, NKJV].

"Go, wash in the pool of Siloam" (John 9)

"Now as Jesus passed by, He saw a man who was blind from birth. And His disciples asked Him, 'Rabbi, who sinned, this man or his parents, that he was born blind?' Jesus answered, 'Neither this man nor his parents sinned, but that the works of God should be revealed in him [other texts read "but let the works of God be displayed in him"]. I must work the works of Him who sent Me while it is day; the night is coming [during the Tribulation] when no one can work. As long as I am in the world, I am the light of the world' [prophecy]. When He had said these things, He spat on the ground and made clay with the saliva; and He anointed the eyes of the blind man with the clay. And He said to him, 'Go, wash in the pool of Siloam' (which is translated Sent) [word of knowledge, word of wisdom, believing faith]. So he went and washed, and came back seeing" [miracle, gift of healing] [John 9:1-7, NKJV].

"Lazarus, come forth!" (John 11)

"Now a certain man was sick, Lazarus of Bethany, the town of Mary and her sister Martha. It was that Mary who anointed the Lord with fragrant oil and wiped His feet with her hair, whose brother Lazarus was sick. Therefore the sisters sent to Him, saying, 'Lord, behold, he whom You love is sick.' When Jesus heard that, He said, 'This sickness is not unto death, but for the glory of God, that the Son of God may be glorified through it' [word of knowledge, word of wisdom, believing faith]. Now Jesus loved Martha and her sister and Lazarus. So that when He heard that he was sick, He stayed two more days in the place where He was [word of wisdom—guidance from His Father]. Then after this He said to the disciples, 'Let us go to Judea again.' The disciples said to Him, 'Rabbi, lately the Jews sought to stone You, and are You going there again?' Jesus answered, 'Are there not twelve hours in the day? If anyone walks in the day, He does not stumble because he sees the light of this world. But if one walks in the night, he stumbles because the light is not in him.' These things He said, and after that He said to them, 'Our friend Lazarus sleeps, but I go that I may wake him up.' Then His disciples said, 'Lord, if he sleeps he will get well.' However, Jesus spoke of his death, but they thought that He was speaking about taking rest in sleep. Then Jesus said to them plainly, 'Lazarus is dead. And I am glad for your sakes that I was not there, that you may believe. Nevertheless let us go to him' [Jesus already understood via revelation from His Father that Lazarus was dead and that He would raise him up]. Then Thomas, who is called the Twin, said to his fellow disciples, 'Let us also go, that we may die with him.'

"So when Jesus came, He found that he had already been in the tomb four days. Now Bethany was near Jerusalem, about two miles away. And many of the Jews had joined the women around Martha and Mary, to comfort them concerning their brother. Then Martha, as soon as she heard that Jesus was coming, went and met Him, but Mary was sitting in the house. Now Martha said to Jesus, 'Lord, if you had been here, my brother would not have died. But even now I know that whatever You ask of God, God will give You.' Jesus said to her, 'Your brother will rise again.' Martha said to Him, 'I know that he will rise again in the resurrection at the last day.' Jesus said to her, 'I am the resurrection and the life. He who believes in Me, though he may die, he shall live. And whoever lives and believes in Me shall never die [prophecy]. Do you believe this?' She said to Him, 'Yes, Lord, I believe You are the Christ, the Son of God, who is to come into the world.' And when she had said these things, she went her way and secretly called Mary her sister, saying, 'The Teacher has come and is calling for you.' As soon as she heard that, she arose quickly and came to Him. Now Jesus had not yet come into the town, but was in the place where Martha met Him. Then the Jews who were with her in the house, and comforting her, when they saw that Mary rose up and quickly went out, followed her, saying, 'She is going to the tomb to weep there.' Then, when Mary came where Jesus was, and saw Him, she fell down at His feet, saying to Him, 'Lord, if You had been here, my brother would not have died.' Therefore, when Jesus saw her weeping, and the Jews who came with her weeping, He groaned in the spirit and was troubled. And He said, 'Where have you laid him?' They said to Him, 'Lord, come and see.' Jesus wept. Then the Jews said, 'See how He loved him!' And some of them said, 'Could not this Man, who opened the eyes of the blind, also have kept this man from dying?' Then Jesus, again groaning in Himself, came to the tomb. It was a cave, and a stone lay against it. Jesus said, 'Take away the stone' [word of knowledge, word of wisdom]. Martha, the sister of him who was dead, said to Him, 'Lord, by this time there is a stench, for he has been dead four days.' Jesus said to her, 'Did I not say to you that if you would believe you would see the glory of God?' Then they took away the stone from the place where the dead man was lying. And Jesus lifted up His eyes and said, 'Father, I thank You that You have heard Me. And I know that You always hear Me, but because of the people who are standing by I said this, that they may believe that You sent Me.' Now when He had said these things, He cried with a loud voice, 'Lazarus, come forth!' [word of knowledge, word of wisdom, believing faith]. And he who had died came out [miracle, gift of healing] bound hand and foot with grave clothes, and his face was wrapped with a cloth. Jesus said to them, 'Loose him, and let him go'" [John 11:1-44, NKJV.

It is perplexing to many readers of the Bible that Jesus "stayed two more days in the place where He was," even when He knew Lazarus was not sleeping but was dead. Why did He not go to Bethany quickly to comfort Mary and Martha and raise Lazarus from the dead, since His Father had already informed Him that He could and would do so? The English Bible scholar E. W. Bullinger, in *The Companion Bible,* writes: "The Jews did not accept evidence as to the identification of a dead body until after three days . . . This period seems, therefore, to have been chosen by the Lord . . . to associate the fact of resurrection with the certainty of death, so as to preclude all doubt that death had actually taken place, and shut out all suggestion that it might have been a trance, or a mere case of resuscitation. The fact that Lazarus had been dead 'four days already' was urged by Martha as a proof that Lazarus was dead, for 'by this time there is a stench'" [Appendix 148].

In his *Commentary on the New Testament From the Talmud and Hebraica—Exercitations Upon the Evangelist St. John, Chapter 11,* the renowned Hebrew scholar John Lightfoot writes: "For he [Lazarus] hath been dead four days . . . The three days of weeping now past, and the four days of lamentation begun: so that all hope and expectation of his coming to himself was wholly gone . . . They [the ruling Sanhedrim] do not certify of the dead (that this is the very man and not another) but within the three days after his decease: for after three days his countenance is changed."

Thus we can understand why Jesus waited until after his beloved friend Lazarus had been dead and in the tomb for *more than three days* before going to raise him from the dead so that the people and the ruling Sanhedrim Council could not claim that it was a hoax. Moreover, this lends much insight into the Lord's prophecy concerning his own death and resurrection: "For as Jonah was three days and three nights [not an idiom meaning any part of three days and three nights: ". . . when the number of 'nights' is stated (in the Bible) as well as the number of 'days,' then the expression ceases to be an idiom, and becomes a literal statement of fact"—*The Companion Bible,* Appendix 144] in the belly of the great fish, so will the Son of Man be three days and three nights in the heart of the earth" [Matthew 12:39, NKJV].

"Cast the net on the right side" (John 21)

"After these things Jesus showed Himself again to the disciples at the Sea of Tiberias, and in this way He showed Himself: Simon Peter, Thomas called the Twin, Nathanial of Cana in Galilee, the sons of Zebedee, and two other of His disciples were together. Simon Peter said to them 'I am going fishing.' They said to him, 'We are going with you also.' They went out and immediately got into the boat, and that night they caught nothing. But when the morning had now come, Jesus stood on the shore; yet the disciples did not know that it was Jesus. Then Jesus said to them 'Children, have you any food?' They answered Him, 'No.' And He said to them, 'Cast the net on the right side of the boat, and you will find some' [word of knowledge, word of wisdom, believing faith]. So they cast, and now they were not able to draw it in because of the multitude of fish [miracle] [John 21:1-6, NKJV].

"you shall receive power" (Acts 1)

"And being assembled together with them, He commanded them not to depart from Jerusalem, but to wait for the Promise of the Father, 'which,' He said, 'you have heard from Me. For John truly baptized with water, but you shall be baptized with the Holy Spirit not many days from now' [word of knowledge, word of wisdom, prophecy]. Therefore, when they had come together, they asked Him, saying, 'Lord, will you at this time restore the kingdom to Israel?' And He said to them, 'It is not for you to know the times or seasons ["the times or dates"—NIV] which the Father has put in His own authority. But you shall receive [*lambano*-"receive into evidence, take possession of"] power [*dunamis*-"inherent ability"] when the Holy Spirit has come upon you, and you shall be witnesses to Me in Jerusalem, and in all Judea and Samaria, and to the end of the earth' [word of knowledge, word of wisdom, prophecy]. Now when He had spoken these things, while they watched, He was taken up, and a cloud received Him out of their sight [miracle, phenomenon]. And while they looked steadfastly toward heaven as He went up, behold, two men stood by them in white apparel [miracle, phenomenon], who also said, 'Men of Galilee, why do you stand gazing up into heaven? This same Jesus, who was taken up from you into heaven, will so come in like manner as you saw Him go into heaven" [prophecy] [Acts 1:4-11, NKJV].

Summary
How did He do it?

During His ministry on earth, Jesus operated seven of the nine manifestations of the spirit which Paul lists in 1 Corinthians 12. And everything He did He did in accordance with His Father's direction by means of the spirit upon Him.

Verse to Remember: "I can do nothing on my own. As I hear, I judge, and my judgment is just, because I seek not my own will but the will of Him who sent me" [John 5:30, ESV].

Questions to ask Myself: Is the fog of mystery lifting for me? Am I beginning to see and understand how Jesus "did it"—"in the power of the spirit"?

Exercise: Every record in the Gospels where Jesus opened the eyes of the blind, healed the sick, made the lame to walk, raised the dead, and healed the brokenhearted is a teachable lesson for those who would be His disciples. Ask yourself: "How does this relate to me? What miracles of deliverance has the Lord performed in my life to show me that He loves me and that He works in me "both to will and to do for His good pleasure"? [Philippians 2:13, NKJV].

ELEVEN

How did His disciples do it?

"**W**hen the Day of Pentecost had fully come, they [the twelve] were all of one accord in one place. And suddenly there came a sound from heaven, as of a rushing mighty wind [phenomenon], and it filled [*pleroo*-"filled to the full'] the whole house where they were sitting. Then there appeared to them divided tongues as of fire, and one sat upon each of them [phenomenon]. And they were all filled [*pletho*-"filled to overflowing"] with the Holy Spirit [the gift] and began to speak with other tongues, as the Spirit [the Lord] gave them utterance" [Acts 2:1- 4, NKJV].

Pentecost marked the original baptism [immersion] in holy spirit—"power from on high"—an early delivery of "the Promise of My Father." For the first time believers in Jesus Christ were "endued [*endyo*-"clothed, arrayed"] with "power" [*dunamis*-"inherent ability"] so that they could be "witnesses" to Jesus "in Jerusalem, and in all Judea and Samaria, and to the end of the earth." Speaking in tongues was the first manifestation of the gift of holy spirit that the disciples of Jesus exhibited. The purpose of the manifestation of speaking in tongues was so that believers could praise God perfectly and persistently—"we hear them speaking in our own tongues the wonderful works of God" [Acts 2:11, NKJV]. As well, believers could now "edify"—build up, strengthen—the gift of the spirit that was "sealed" in them—"you were sealed with the Holy Spirit [the gift] of promise" [Ephesians 1:13, NKJV].

Immediately prior to Pentecost, Simon Peter and the other disciples of Jesus were in hiding—shut behind locked doors "for fear of the Jews" [John 20:19, NKJV]. What changed Peter? It was the baptism in holy spirit, the *conviction* that what Jesus had promised—"I will not leave you orphans, I will come to you"—and "At that day you will know [*ginosko*-"perceive, understand, know by personal experience"] that I am in My Father, and you in Me, and I in you"—He had personally delivered! [John 14:18,20, NKJV].

Peter immediately demonstrated the power and presence of the gift of holy spirit—"Christ in you"—in perhaps the most persuasive speech [prophecy] recorded in the Bible: ". . . Peter, standing up with the eleven, raised his voice and said to them, 'Men of Judea and all who dwell in Jerusalem, let this be known to you, and heed my words . . . Jesus of Nazareth, a Man attested by God to you by miracles, wonders, and signs which God did through Him in your midst, as you yourselves also know—Him, being delivered by the determined purpose and foreknowledge of God, you have taken by lawless hands, have crucified, and put to death, whom God raised up, because it was not possible that He should be held by it . . . This Jesus God has raised up, of which we are all witnesses. Therefore being exalted to the right hand of God, and having received from the Father the promise of the Holy Spirit [the gift], He poured out this which you now see and hear . . . Therefore let all the house of Israel know that God has made this Jesus, whom you crucified, both Lord and Christ" [Acts 2:22,32,36, NKJV].

The record continues: "Now when they heard this, they were cut to the heart, and said to Peter and the rest of the apostles, 'Men and brethren, what shall we do?' Then Peter said to them, 'Repent [change your mind] and let every one of you be baptized in the name of Jesus Christ for the remission of sins; and you shall receive [*lambano*-"receive into evidence"] the gift of the Holy Spirit. For the promise is to you and to your children, and to all who are afar off; as many as the Lord our God will call.' And with many other words he testified and exhorted them, saying, 'Be saved from this perverse generation.' And those who gladly received his word were baptized; and that day about three thousand souls were added to them" [Acts 2:37-41, NKJV].

From that day forward, Peter was a changed man—a man of focus, purpose, and holy spirit authority. "Now Peter and John went up together to the temple at the hour of prayer, the ninth hour. And a certain man lame from his mother's womb was carried, whom they laid daily at the gate of the temple which is called Beautiful, to ask alms from those who entered the temple, who, seeing Peter and John about to go into the temple, asked for alms. And fixing his eyes on him, with John, Peter said, 'Look at us.' So he gave them his attention, expecting to receive something from them. [No doubt Peter and John had been speaking in tongues much since Pentecost, effectively edifying the spirit born in them, so that they were prepared to obey the Lord when He spoke to them.] Then Peter said, 'Silver and gold I do not have, but what I do have I give you: In the name of Jesus Christ of Nazareth, rise up and walk' [revelation from the Lord: word of knowledge, word of wisdom, believing faith]. And he took him by the right hand and lifted him up, and immediately his feet and ankle bones received strength [miracle, gift of healing]. So he, leaping up, stood and walked and entered the temple with them—walking, leaping, and praising God. And all the people saw him walking and praising God. Then they knew that it was he who sat begging alms at the Beautiful Gate of the temple; and they were filled with wonder and amazement at what had happened to him" [Acts 3:1-10, NKJV].

The manifestations of the spirit and the accompanying signs, miracles, and wonders from the Lord are intended to arrest people's attention to the word of God being spoken, to glorify God by "setting the captives free," and to lead those who believe to salvation that is by faith in Jesus Christ.

"one heart and one soul" (Acts 4)

Following the miraculous healing of the man lame from his mother's womb, "all the people ran together to them in the porch which is called Solomon's greatly amazed" [Acts 3:11, NKJV]. Again Peter responded with inspired preaching of God's word to such a degree that "the priests, the captain of the temple, and the Sadducees came upon them, being greatly disturbed that they taught the people and preached in Jesus the resurrection from the dead. And they laid hands on them, and put them in custody until the next day, for it was already evening. However many of those who heard the word believed; and the number of the men came to be about five thousand" [Acts 4:1-4]. "So faith comes from hearing, and hearing through the word of Christ" [Romans 10:17, ESV].

The next day Peter and John are brought before the "rulers, elders, and scribes, as well as Annas the high priest, Caiaphas, John, and Alexander, and as many as were the family of the high priest in Jerusalem" [vss. 5a,6]. Once again Peter responds with inspired utterance and prophecy. Eventually they were threatened and commanded "not to speak nor teach at all in the name of Jesus." But Peter and John answered them: "Whether it is right in the sight of God to listen to you more than to God, you judge. For we cannot but speak the things which we have seen and heard" [vss. 18-20]. "And being let go, they went to their own companions and reported all that the chief priests and elders had said to them" [v. 23].

There they rejoiced with the believers and prayed together, saying, "Now, Lord, look on their threats, and grant to your servants that with all boldness they may speak your word, by stretching out your hand to heal, and that signs and wonders may be done through the name of your holy servant Jesus. And when they had prayed, the place where they were assembled together was shaken [phenomenon] and they were all filled [*pimplemi*-"to the full"] with the Holy Spirit [the gift], and they spoke the word of God with boldness. Now the multitude of those who believed were of one heart [*kardia*-"center of one's personal life"] and soul [*psyche*-"seat of the feelings, affections"]; neither did anyone say that any of the things that he possessed was his own, but they had all things in common. And with great power [*dunamis*] the apostles gave witness [by means of the manifestations of the spirit] to the resurrection of the Lord Jesus. And great grace was upon them all" [vss. 29-33].

"Now the multitude of those who believed were of one heart and one soul . . . ." This is a figure of speech, more specifically: "the heart and the soul one," indicating great unity of faith and purpose. No church or fellowship of believers will ever accomplish much in terms of exhibiting the "great grace" of the presence of the living Christ unless and until they are "of one heart and one soul." And it is not possible for a congregation of believers to achieve this degree of unity that we see in Acts 4 unless they are taught the accuracy of God's word, specifically "the Lord's curriculum," by the pastors and teachers in the group. Without this plan in operation, the group will be spiritually weak—like most churches today which practice spiritually impotent religion instead of the truth that sets people free. In Revelation 3:14 the Lord says to the church of the Laodiceans: "I know your works, that you are neither hot nor cold. I could wish you were cold or hot. So then, because you are lukewarm, and neither cold nor hot, I will vomit you out of My mouth" [NKJV]. The Lord is not pleased with a "lukewarm" church!

". . . and they were all healed." (Acts 5)

"And through the hands of the apostles many signs and wonders were done among the people. And they were all with one accord [great unity of believing faith] in Solomon's Porch. Yet none of the rest dared join them, but the people esteemed them highly. And believers were increasingly added [born again] to the Lord, multitudes of both men and women [because of the signs and wonders by means of the manifestations of the spirit confirming the resurrection of the Lord] so that they brought the sick out into the streets and laid them on beds and couches, that at least the shadow of Peter passing by might fall on some of them. Also a multitude gathered from the surrounding cities to Jerusalem, bringing sick people and those who were tormented by unclean spirits, and they were all healed" [words of knowledge, words of wisdom, discerning of spirits, believing faith, miracles, gifts of healing working in process in the disciples] [Acts 5:12-16, NKJV].

Again we recognize the great faith and expectation of the Lord's living presence in and among the believers—great "unity of the spirit"—so that "many signs and wonders" were accomplished among the people by the hands of the apostles. The believers were congregating regularly in "Solomon's Portico," hearing the apostles' inspired teaching of God's word, manifesting the spirit by speaking in tongues with interpretation and prophesying, rejoicing together in the reality of the Lord's pouring out "power from on high." They did not doubt God's ability and willingness to heal, and so "they were all healed."

"Stephen, full of faith . . ." (Acts 6)

"Then the word of God spread, and the number of the disciples multiplied greatly in Jerusalem, and a great many of the priests were obedient to the faith. And Stephen [a deacon], full of faith and power [*dunamis*], did great wonders and signs [words of knowledge, words of wisdom, believing faith, miracles] among the people" [Acts 6:8, NKJV].

Philip in Samaria (Acts 8)

"Then Philip went down to the city of Samaria and preached Christ to them. And the multitude of one accord heeded the things spoken by Philip, hearing and seeing the miracles which he did [by means of *dunamis* and the manifestations of words of knowledge, words of wisdom, discerning of spirits, believing faith, miracles, gifts of healing]. For unclean spirits, crying with a loud voice, came out of many who were possessed; and many who were paralyzed and lame were healed. And there was great joy in that city. But there was a certain man called Simon, who previously practiced sorcery in the city and astonished the people of Samaria, claiming that he was someone great, to whom they all gave heed, from the least to the greatest, saying, 'This man is the great power of God.' And they heeded him because he had astonished them with his sorceries for a long time. But when they believed Philip as he preached the things concerning the kingdom of God and the name of Jesus Christ, both men and women were baptized. Then Simon himself also believed; and when he was baptized he continued with Philip, and was amazed, seeing the miracles and signs which were done" [Acts 8:5-13, NKJV].

What did Simon see? (Acts 8)

"Now when the apostles who were at Jerusalem heard that Samaria had received [*dechomai*-"received favorably"] the word of God, they sent Peter and John to them [two pillars of the church, sent to Samaria because suddenly there was no evidencing of the gift of holy spirit when the people believed], who, when they had come down, prayed for them that they might receive [*lambano*-"receive into evidence"] the Holy Spirit. For yet He [the gift] had fallen [in the evidence of speaking in tongues and prophesying] on none of them. They had only been baptized [into the faith] in the name of the Lord. Then they laid hands on them [in prayer for the operation of the manifestations of the spirit], and they [the new believers] received [*lambano*-"into evidence"] the Holy Spirit. And when Simon saw that through the laying on of the apostles' hands the Holy Spirit was given [he saw the manifestation of speaking in tongues and/or prophesying], he offered them money, saying, 'Give me this power also, that anyone on whom I lay my hands may receive [*lambano*-"into evidence"] the Holy Spirit.' But Peter said to him, 'Your money perish with you, because you thought that the gift of God could be purchased with money'" [Acts 8:14-19,NKJV].

The baptism in holy spirit—the gift of God—is by God's grace: "For by grace you have been saved through faith, and that not of yourselves; it is the gift of God, not of works, lest anyone should boast" [Ephesians 2:8, NKJV]. And the resulting manifestations of the spirit are for God's glory and the furthering of the gospel. They must be operated in love: "Though I speak with the tongues of men and of angels, but have not love [*agape*], I have become sounding brass or a clanging symbol [MSG: "nothing but the creaking of a rusty gate"]. And though I have the gift of prophecy ["the gift of" is not in the Greek text] and understand all mysteries and all knowledge, and though I have all faith so that I could remove mountains, but have not love, I am nothing" [1 Corinthians 13:1,2, NKJV].

"a certain disciple at Damascus" (Acts 9)

"Now there was a certain disciple [not an apostle, not a prophet, just a faithful believer] at Damascus named Ananias; and to him the Lord said in a vision [word of knowledge, word of wisdom], 'Ananias.' And he said, 'Here I am, Lord.' So the Lord said to him, 'Arise and go to the street called Straight, and inquire at the house of Judas for one called Saul of Tarsus, for behold, he is praying. And in a vision he has seen [word of knowledge] a man named Ananias coming in and putting his hand on him, so that he might receive [*anablepo*-"recover"] his sight.' Then Ananias answered, 'Lord, I have heard from many about this man, how much harm he has done to Your saints in Jerusalem. And here he has authority from the chief priests to bind all who call on Your name.' But the Lord said to him, 'Go, for he is a chosen vessel of Mine to bear My name before Gentiles, kings, and the children of Israel. For I will show him how many things he must suffer for My name's sake.'

"And Ananias went his way and entered the house, and laying his hands on him [word of knowledge, word of wisdom, believing faith], he said, 'Brother Saul, the Lord Jesus, who appeared to you on the road as you came, has sent me that you may receive [recover] your sight and be filled [*pletho*-"filled to overflowing"] with the Holy Spirit' [the gift]. Immediately there fell from his eyes something like scales, and he received his sight at once [miracle, gift of healing]; and he arose and was baptized" [Acts 9:10-18,NKJV]. Saul was "filled to overflowing" with holy spirit; that is to say, he manifested.

"Jesus the Christ heals you" (Acts 9)

"Now it came to pass, as Peter went through all parts of the country, that he also came down to the saints who dwelt in Lydda. There he found a certain man named Aeneas, who had been bedridden eight years and was paralyzed. And Peter said to him, 'Aeneas, Jesus Christ heals you. Arise and make your bed' [word of knowledge, word of wisdom, believing faith]. Then he arose immediately [miracle, gift of healing]. So all who dwelt at Lydda and Sharon saw him and turned to the Lord" [Acts 9:32-35, NKJV].

"Tabitha, arise" (Acts 9)

"At Joppa there was a certain disciple named Tabitha, which is translated Dorcas. This woman was full of good works and charitable deeds which she did. But it happened in those days that she became sick and died. When they had washed her, they laid her in an upper room. And since Lydda was near Joppa, and the disciples had heard that Peter was there, they sent two men to him, imploring him not to delay in coming to them. Then Peter arose and went with them. When he had come, they brought him to the upper room. And all the widows stood by him weeping, showing the tunics and garments which Dorcas had made while she was with them. But Peter put them all out, and knelt down and prayed [thanking the Lord for the operation of the manifestations of the spirit]. And turning to the body he said, 'Tabitha, arise' [word of knowledge, word of wisdom, believing faith]. And she opened her eyes, and when she saw Peter she sat up [miracle, gift of healing]. Then he gave her his hand and lifted her up; and when he had called the saints and widows, he presented her alive. And it became known throughout all Joppa, and many believed on the Lord" [Acts 9:36-42, NKJV].

Peter at the house of Cornelius (Acts 10)

"There was a certain man in Caesarea called Cornelius, a centurion of what was called the Italian Regiment, a devout man and one who feared God and all his household, who gave alms generously to the people, and prayed to God always. About the ninth hour of the day he saw clearly in a vision an angel of God coming in and saying to him, 'Cornelius!' [word of knowledge, word of wisdom—and indeed a phenomenon because not all revelation from the Lord is delivered by an angel!] [Acts 10:1-3, NKJV].

As it happened, Cornelius is inspired by the angel to send for Peter who is staying with Simon whose house is by the sea. Soon after, Peter, while he is up on the roof in prayer, "fell into a trance [*ekstasis*-"a rapt vision"] [word of knowledge, word of wisdom] and saw heaven opened and an object like a great sheet bound at the four corners, descending to him and let down to the earth" [vss. 10b, 11]. In the vision, the Lord shows Peter animals, creeping things, and birds—"unclean" according to Jewish law—in order to make the point that "What God has cleansed you must not call common" [v. 15]. This was done three times. "Now while Peter wondered within himself what this vision which he had seen meant, behold, the men who had been sent from Cornelius had made inquiry for Simon's house and stood before the gate. And they called and asked whether Simon, whose surname was Peter, was lodging there. While Peter thought about the vision, the Spirit said to him [word of knowledge, word of wisdom], 'Behold, three men are seeking you. Arise therefore, go down and go with them, doubting nothing; for I have sent them'" [vss. 15b-20].

Peter is encouraged by the visitors to go to Caesarea to the house of Cornelius. When he arrives, he finds "many who had come together" [v. 27], for Cornelius "had called together his relatives and close friends . . . to hear all the things commanded you by God" [vss. 24, 33b]. "Then Peter opened his mouth and said, 'In truth I perceive that God shows no partiality. But in every nation whoever fears Him and works righteousness is accepted by Him. The word which God sent to the children of Israel, preaching peace through Jesus Christ—He is Lord of all— that word you know, which was proclaimed throughout all Judea, and began from Galilee after the baptism which John preached: how God anointed Jesus of Nazareth with the Holy Spirit [the fullness] and with power, who went about doing good and healing all who were oppressed by the devil, for God was with Him" [inspired teaching, prophecy] [vss. 34-38].

Peter continued to teach and preach to the household of Cornelius, and while he "was still speaking these words, the Holy Spirit fell upon all those who heard the word [phenomenon]. And those of the circumcision who believed were astonished, as many as came with Peter, because the gift of the Holy Spirit had been poured out on the Gentiles also. For they heard them speak with tongues and magnify God. Then Peter answered, 'Can anyone forbid water, that these should not be baptized who have received [lambano-"into evidence"] the Holy Spirit just as we have?' [vss. 44-47]. [It is clear that Peter did not yet understand that water baptism was no longer a requirement for ritual "cleansing," as it was under the Law; for he did not fully comprehend at this time that "Christ is the end of the law for righteousness to everyone who believes" [Romans 10:4, NKJV]. This truth the Lord revealed to Paul years later].

"Saul . . . filled with the Holy Spirit" (Acts 13)

"Now in the church that was at Antioch there were certain prophets and teachers: Barnabas, Simeon who was called Niger, Lucius of Cyrene, Manaen who had been brought up with Herod the tetrarch, and Saul. As they ministered to the Lord and fasted, the Holy Spirit [God] said, 'Now separate to Me Barnabas and Saul for the work to which I have called them' [word of knowledge, word of wisdom]. Then, having fasted and prayed, and laid hands on them [for prophecy], they sent them away. So, being sent out by the Holy Spirit [God], they went down to Seleucia, and from there they sailed to Cyprus. And when they arrived in Salamis, they preached the word of God in the synagogue of the Jews. They also had John as their assistant.

"Now when they had gone through the island of Paphos, they found a certain sorcerer, a false prophet, whose name was Bar-jesus, who was with the proconsul, Sergius Paulus, an intelligent man. This man called for Barnabas and Saul and sought to hear the word of God. But Elymas the sorcerer (for so his name is translated) withstood them, seeking to turn the proconsul away from the faith. Then Saul, who also is called Paul, filled [pimplemi-"to the full"] with the Holy Spirit [the gift], looked intently at him and said, 'O full of all deceit and all fraud, you son of the devil, you enemy of all righteousness, will you not cease perverting the straight ways of the Lord? And now, indeed, the hand of the Lord is upon you, and you shall be blind, not seeing the sun for a time' [word of knowledge, word of wisdom, discerning of spirits, believing faith]. And immediately a dark mist fell on him [miracle, phenomenon], and he went around seeking someone to lead him by the hand. Then the proconsul believed, when he saw what had been done, being astonished at the teaching of the Lord" [Acts 13:1-12, NKJV].

"The gods have come down to us!" (Acts 14)

"Now it happened in Iconium that they went together to the synagogue of the Jews, and so spoke that a great multitude both of the Jews and the Greeks believed. But the unbelieving Jews stirred up the Gentiles and poisoned their minds against the brethren. Therefore they stayed there a long time, speaking boldly in the Lord [they did not abandon the new believers to the persecutions of the enemy] who was bearing witness to the word of His grace, granting signs and wonders to be done by their hands."

This is an important point. The Lord was "granting [*didomi*-"furnishing, supplying, delivering"] signs and wonders to be done by their hands." A believer can operate the manifestations of speaking in tongues, interpretation of tongues, and prophecy any time he chooses. However, when it comes to the revelation manifestations—word of knowledge, word of wisdom, discerning of spirits—and the power (or impartation) manifestations—working of miracles and gifts of healing—it is entirely up to the Lord's love and grace in any given situation to provide the knowledge and the wisdom and then to "activate" the *dunamis*—the spiritual energy—in the believer necessary for the miracle or healing to come to pass according to the believer's absolute faith for Him to do so. The Lord will normally not do this in a believer who is vacillating, what James calls "a double-minded man, unstable in all his ways . . . let not that man suppose that he will receive anything from the Lord" [James 1:7, 8, NKJV]. Paul was not a "vacillating" believer. He was operating in the spiritual "office" of an apostle. Ephesians 4 tells us that "When He [Christ] ascended on high, He led captivity captive, and gave gifts to men" [v. 8]. Then in verses 11 and 12: "And He Himself gave some to be apostles, some prophets, some evangelists, and some pastors and teachers, for the equipping of the saints for the work of the ministry, for the edifying of the body of Christ . . ." [NKJV]. These are the "gift ministries" in the Body. The "gifts" are the lives of the individuals in dedicated service to the Lord; they are not special abilities or endowments of power. A person with a "gift ministry" from the Lord has no more "anointing" than any other believer, no additional "Christ in you." However, because of their spiritual maturity, faith and commitment to obeying the Lord, they may indeed operate the manifestations of the spirit more efficaciously than other believers, with the Lord "granting signs and wonders to be done by their hands."

Along with the "gift ministries" in the Body of Christ, there are other spiritual "gifts and callings." Paul says in 1 Corinthians 12:4, NKJV, that "There are diversities of gifts [*charisma*-"favor with which one receives without any merit on his own"], but the same Spirit" [the gift of holy spirit]. "For as in one body we have many members, and the members do not all have the same function, so we, though many, are one body in Christ, and individually members one of another. Having gifts [*charisma*] that differ according to the grace given to us, let us use them: if prophecy, in proportion to our faith [Paul is not talking here about a "gift" of prophecy—he is simply saying that some believers may excel at prophesying according to the proportion of their faith]; if service, in our serving; the one who teaches, in his teaching; the one who exhorts, in his exhortation; the one who contributes, in generosity; the one who leads, with zeal; the one who does acts of mercy, with cheerfulness" [Romans 12:4-8, ESV]. Our Heavenly Father knows each one of His children better than we know ourselves. He knows who will excel at prophesying, who will excel at teaching, or exhorting, or giving, or leading, etc. And so He works in each one of us to help us to develop our natural abilities in correspondence with the spirit born in us in order to best serve the whole Body. Peter says: "As each has received a gift [*charisma*], use it to serve one another, as good stewards of God's varied grace . . ." [1 Peter 4:10, ESV]. It is a "gift" in the sense that the Lord puts it on the heart of the believer to serve in a special way and then energizes the believer's endeavors as he proceeds.

"But the multitude of the city was divided: part sided with the Jews, and part with the apostles. And when a violent attempt was made by both the Gentiles and Jews, with their rulers, to abuse and stone them, they became aware of it and fled to Lystra and Derbe, cities of Lyconia, and to the surrounding region. And they were preaching the gospel there. And in Lystra a certain man without strength in his feet was sitting, a cripple from his mother's womb, who had never walked. This man heard Paul speaking. Paul, observing him intently, and seeing that he had faith to be healed [word of knowledge, word of wisdom, believing faith], said with a loud voice, 'Stand up straight on your feet!' And he leaped and walked [faith meeting faith: miracle, gift of healing]. Now when the people saw what Paul had done, they raised their voices, saying in the Lycaonian language, 'The gods have come down to us in the likeness of men!'" [Acts 14:1-11, NKJV].

". . . a spirit of divination" (Acts 16)

"Now it happened, as we went to prayer [it is interesting to note that here Luke joins Paul on his journey and begins to write in the first person], a certain slave girl possessed with a spirit of divination met us, who brought her masters much profit by fortune-telling. This girl followed Paul and us, and cried out, saying, 'These men are the servants of the most high God, who proclaim to us the way of salvation.' And this she did for many days. But Paul, greatly annoyed, turned and said to the spirit, 'I command you in the name of Jesus Christ to come out of her' [word of knowledge, word of wisdom, discerning of spirits, believing faith]. And he [it] came out that very hour" [miracle, gift of healing]. [Acts 16:16-18, NKJV].

"Did you receive the Holy Spirit when you believed?" (Acts 19)

"And it happened, while Apollos was at Corinth [having recently been in Ephesus teaching only "the baptism of John"—Acts 18:25], that Paul, having passed through the upper regions, came to Ephesus. And finding some disciples, he said to them, 'Did you receive [*lambano*-"receive into evidence"] the Holy Spirit when you believed?' So they said to him, 'We have not so much as heard whether there is a Holy Spirit.' And he said to them, 'Into what then were you baptized?' So they said, 'Into John's baptism.' Then Paul said, 'John indeed baptized with a baptism of repentance, saying to the people that they should believe on Him who would come after him, that is, on Christ Jesus.' When they heard this, they were baptized in the name of the Lord Jesus. And when Paul had laid hands on them [word of knowledge, word of wisdom], the Holy Spirit [the gift] came upon them, and they spoke with tongues and prophesied . . . ."

"Now God worked unusual miracles by the hands of Paul, so that even handkerchiefs or aprons were brought from his body to the sick, and the diseases left them [miracles, gifts of healing, phenomena] and the evil spirits went out of them" [Acts 19:1-6, 11,12, NKJV].

"a certain prophet named Agabus" (Acts 21)

"When we had sighted Cyprus, we passed it on the left, sailed to Syria, and landed at Tyre; for there the ship was to unload her cargo. And finding disciples, we stayed there seven days. They told Paul through the Spirit [the gift] not to go up to Jerusalem [word of knowledge, word of wisdom, prophecy] . . . And when we had finished our voyage from Tyre, we came to Ptolemais, greeted the brethren, and stayed with them one day. On the next day we who were Paul's companions departed and came to Caesarea, and entered the house of Philip the evangelist, who was one of the seven, and stayed with him. Now this man had four virgin daughters who prophesied. And as we stayed many days, a certain prophet name Agabus came down from Judea. When he had come to us, he took Paul's belt, bound his own hands and feet, and said, 'Thus says the Holy Spirit [God], So shall the Jews at Jerusalem bind the man who owns this belt, and deliver him into the hands of the Gentiles'" [word of knowledge, word of wisdom, prophecy]. Now when we heard these things, both we and those from that place pleaded with him not to go up to Jerusalem. Then Paul answered, 'What do you mean by weeping and breaking my heart? For I am ready not only to be bound, but also to die at Jerusalem for the name of the Lord Jesus. So when he would not be persuaded, we ceased, saying, 'The will of the Lord be done.'" [Clearly the will of the Lord, via prophecy, was that Paul not go to Jerusalem. In most versions of the Bible, the comma after the word "ceased" is erroneously supplied. The prophets were informing Paul of the Lord's will. When he stubbornly refused to be persuaded, they ceased trying to convince him not to go to Jerusalem. The next chapters describe what hardships and frustrations befell Paul when he refused the will of the Lord. Nevertheless the Lord's grace and mercy continued to be magnified in his ministry] [Acts 21:3,4,7-14, NKJV].

Paul on Malta (Acts 28)

"Now when they had escaped, they then found out that the island was called Malta. And the natives showed us unusual kindness; for they kindled a fire and made us all welcome, because of the rain that was falling and because of the cold. But when Paul had gathered a bundle of sticks and laid them on the fire, a viper came out because of the heat, and fastened on his hand. So when the natives saw the creature hanging from his hand, they said to one another, 'No doubt this man is a murderer, whom, though he has escaped the sea, yet justice does not allow to live.' But he shook off the creature into the fire, and suffered no harm [word of knowledge, word of wisdom, believing faith, miracle, gift of healing]. However, they were expecting that he would suddenly swell up or fall down dead. But after they had looked for a long time and saw no harm come to him, they changed their minds and said that he was a god.

"In that region there was an estate of the leading citizen of the island, whose name was Publius, who received us and entertained us courteously for three days. And it happened that the father of Publius lay sick of a fever and dysentery. Paul went in to him and prayed, and he laid his hands on him and healed him [word of knowledge, word of wisdom, believing faith, gift of healing]. So when this was done, the rest of those on the island who had diseases also came and were healed" [words of knowledge, words of wisdom, believing faith, discerning of spirits, miracles, gifts of healing] [Acts 28:1-9, NKJV].

". . . demonstration of the Spirit" (1 Corinthians 2)

"And I, brethren, when I came to you, did not come with excellence of speech or of wisdom declaring to you the testimony of God. For I determined not to know anything among you except Jesus Christ and Him crucified. I was with you in meekness, in fear, and in much trembling. And my speech and my preaching were not with persuasive words of human wisdom, but in demonstration of the Spirit [the gift] and of power [*dunamis*] [words of knowledge, words of wisdom, prophecy, discerning of spirits, believing faith, miracles, gifts of healing] that your faith should not be in the wisdom of men but in the power [*dunamis*] of God" [1 Corinthians 2:4,5, NKJV].

"caught up into Paradise" (2 Corinthians 12)

"It is doubtless not profitable for me to boast. I will come to visions and revelations of the Lord: I know a man in Christ who fourteen years ago—whether in the body I do not know, or whether out of the body I do not know—such a one was caught up to the third heaven. And I know such a man—whether in the body or out of the body I do not know, God knows—how he was caught up into Paradise and heard inexpressible words, which it is not lawful for a man to utter [word of knowledge, word of wisdom, phenomenon]. Of such a one I will boast; yet of myself I will not boast, except in my infirmities. For though I might desire to boast, I will not be a fool; for I will speak the truth. But I refrain, lest anyone should think of me above what he sees me to be or hears from me. And lest I should be exalted above measure by the abundance of the revelations, a thorn in the flesh was given to me, a messenger of Satan to buffet me [word of knowledge, word of wisdom, discerning of spirits] lest I be exalted above measure. Concerning this thing I pleaded with the Lord three times that it might depart from me. And He said to me, 'My grace is sufficient for you, for My strength ["Christ in you"] is made perfect in weakness' [word of knowledge, word of wisdom]. Therefore most gladly I will rather boast in my infirmities, that the power of Christ may rest upon me. Therefore I take pleasure in infirmities, in reproaches, in needs, in persecutions, in distresses, for Christ's sake. For when I am weak, then I am strong ["I can do all things through Christ who strengthens me"—Philippians 4:13, NKJV]. I have become a fool in boasting; you have compelled me. For I ought to have been commended by you; for in nothing was I behind the most eminent apostles, though I am nothing. Truly the signs of an apostle were accomplished among you with all perseverance, in signs and wonders and mighty deeds" [by means of words of knowledge, words of wisdom, discerning of spirits, believing faith, working of miracles, gifts of healing and *dunamis*] [2 Corinthians 12:1-12, NKJV].

". . . the trumpet of God" (1 Thessalonians 4)

"But we do not want you to be uninformed, brothers, about those who are asleep [having died], that you may not grieve as others do who have no hope. For since we believe that Jesus died and rose again, even so, through Jesus, God will bring with him [at the Rapture of the Church] those who have fallen asleep. For this we declare to you by a word from the Lord [word of knowledge, word of wisdom], that we who are alive, who are left until the coming of the Lord, will not precede those who have fallen asleep. For the Lord himself will descend from heaven with a cry of command, with the voice of an archangel, and with the sound of the trumpet of God. And the dead in Christ will rise first. Then we who are alive, who are left, will be caught up together with them in the clouds to meet the Lord in the air, and so we will always be with the Lord. Therefore encourage one another with these words" [prophecy] [1 Thessalonians 4:13-18, ESV].

Paul says: ". . . and so we will always be with the Lord." The Lord is the head of the Body of Christ, and believers are the members of His Body. After the Rapture of the Church when believers "meet the Lord in the air," then comes the judgment seat of Christ where believers receive rewards for their faithful service to the Lord in this mortal life. Afterwards, when the Lord returns to this earth to "consume [*analisko*—"destroy"] the lawless one" with "the breath [*pneuma*—"spirit"] of His mouth and destroy [*katargeo*—"inactivate, deprive of force, influence, power"] with the brightness of His coming" [2 Thessalonians 2:8, NKJV] and then to establish His Millennial Kingdom, all believers who have been "raptured" return with Him to earth to help in the establishment of His kingdom: "Now Enoch, the seventh from Adam, prophesied about these men also, saying, 'Behold, the Lord comes with ten thousands of His saints'" [*hagios*-"most holy thing, holy ones"]. Also, Paul says: "And may the Lord make you increase and abound in love to one another and to all, just as we do to you, so that He may establish your hearts blameless in holiness before our God and Father at the coming of our Lord Jesus Christ with all His saints" [*hagios*] [1 Thessalonians 3:13, NKJV]. Christians who believe they will spend eternity up in heaven with the Lord are mistaken.

"If any of you lacks wisdom . . ."

When Jesus ministered healing or worked some other miracle to bring deliverance to the oppressed, He never asked His Father to do the healing or if it was His Father's will to heal. Jesus was in constant communion with His Father, praying, talking with Him, listening for guidance in every situation. When a person came to Him in need, He simply proceeded to minister to the person according to the knowledge and wisdom His Father supplied, knowing that He had the *dunamis* and the *exousia* to carry out His Father's will. For example, in Matthew 8 "a leper came and worshipped Him, saying, 'Lord, if you are willing, You can make me clean.' Then Jesus put out His hand and touched Him [word of knowledge, word of wisdom from the Father], saying, 'I am willing; be cleansed'" [vss. 2,3, NKJV]. Jesus knew that God is always willing to heal and deliver according to a person's believing faith.

Likewise, in Acts 9 when the disciples informed Peter that a believer named Tabitha had died, "then Peter arose and went with them. When he had come, they brought him to the upper room . . . But Peter put them all out and knelt down and prayed [Peter was simply thanking the Lord for the knowledge and wisdom he needed to handle the situation.]. And turning to the body he said, 'Tabitha, arise.' And she opened her eyes. And when she saw Peter she sat up" [vss. 39,40, NKJV]. Peter never said, 'Lord, I hope you will raise her. I hope you will do it." No. He knew he was the Lord's representative and he simply acted on the *dunamis* and *exousia* he knew he had in the name of Jesus Christ and according to the knowledge and wisdom the Lord provided.

Likewise, when Paul was in Lystra, "a certain man without strength in his feet was sitting, a cripple from his mother's womb, who had never walked. This man heard Paul speaking. Paul, observing him intently and seeing he had faith to be healed, said with a loud voice, 'Stand up straight on your feet!' And he leaped and walked" [14:8,9, NKJV]. Did Paul pray, "Lord, if it be your will . . . ?" No. He simply acted in believing faith according to the knowledge and wisdom the Lord supplied, knowing he was representing Jesus Christ and that he had the *dunamis* and *exousia* to heal according to the Lord's guidance.

Therefore, in the laying on of hands for the purpose of ministering deliverance to the oppressed, it is imperative to be in prayer and communion with the Father and to ask Him "what to do." James 1:5 says: "If any of you lacks wisdom [what to do!], let him ask of God, who gives to all liberally and without reproach, and it will be given him" [NKJV]. Jesus and His apostles were in continual fellowship [*koinonia*—"communion"] with the Father and had learned by experience that God would provide the wisdom at every opportunity.

The ministry of our Lord Jesus Christ was authenticated by the signs, miracles, and wonders which He did. The signs, miracles, and wonders confirmed the word He taught and attracted the multitudes to hear Him. After He raised His friend Lazarus from the dead, as He entered Jerusalem prior to Passover, "a great multitude that had come to the feast, when they heard that Jesus was coming to Jerusalem, took branches of palm trees and went out to meet Him, and cried out: 'Hosanna! Blessed is He who comes in the name of the Lord' . . .The Pharisees therefore said among themselves, 'You see that you are accomplishing nothing. Look, the world has gone after Him!'" [John 12:12, 13, 19, NKJV].

Likewise, the signs, miracles, and wonders which the apostles and other disciples of Jesus did attracted multitudes to hear the word which they spoke: "So faith comes from hearing, and hearing through the word of Christ" [Romans 10:11, ESV]. The signs, miracles, and wonders the Lord makes available to His faithful disciples today not only demonstrate our Heavenly Father's mercy and great love for His children, they are intended also to attract people to the gospel of Jesus Christ spoken by His disciples so as "to bring many sons and daughters to glory" [Hebrews 2:10, NIV]. The many teachable lessons of deliverance in the Acts of the Apostles confirmed the word of God and, as the result: "So mightily grew the word of God and prevailed" [Acts 19:20, KJV].

Summary
How did His disciples do it?

The manifestations of the spirit and the accompanying signs and wonders are intended to arrest peoples' attention to the word of God being spoken, to glorify God by "setting the captives free," and to lead those who believe to the salvation that is by faith in Jesus Christ.

Verse to Remember: "Now, Lord, . . . grant to Your servants that with all boldness they may speak Your word, by stretching out Your hand to heal, and that signs and wonders may be done through the name of Your holy Servant Jesus" [Acts 4:29,30, NKJV].

Question to ask Myself: What should I be asking the Lord in prayer—persistently if need be—in order to strengthen myself spiritually and guide myself in the way He would have me go?

Exercise: Take the Lord at His word. In prayer, remind Him often of His promises: "I am the Lord who heals you;" "He who believes in Me, the works that I do shall he do also;" "If you ask anything in My name, I will do it;" "And nothing will be impossible for you." It is not being impertinent to remind Him of His promises—it is being proactive in faith: "Let us therefore come boldly to the throne of grace, that we may obtain mercy and find grace to help in time of need" [Hebrews 4:16, NKJV].

TWELVE

How can believers do it today?

The Lord Jesus Christ made an astonishing promise to His disciples two thousand years ago that still rings true today: "Truly, truly, I say to you, whoever believes in me will also do the works that I do; and greater works than these will he do, because I am going to the Father. Whatever you ask in my name, this I will do, that the Father may be glorified in the Son. If you ask me anything in my name, I will do it. If you love me, you will keep my commandments" [John 14:12-15, ESV].

It has been said in various ways by many thoughtful instructors of the Bible that the degree to which we effectively exercise the authority of Christ in us is enhanced by the degree of intimacy we have nurtured and which we cherish with our Heavenly Father and with our Lord Jesus Christ. Following the miraculous healing of the man lame from his mother's womb at the Beautiful Gate of the temple, Peter and John boldly preached Jesus Christ and His resurrection from the dead to the people in the temple square. And "when they saw the boldness of Peter and John, and perceived that they were uneducated and untrained men, they marveled. And they realized that they had been with Jesus" [Acts 4:13, NKJV].

Do people see in us that we "have been with Jesus?" He said: "I am the vine, you are the branches; He who abides in Me [remains, sojourns, lives, continues, endures], and I in him, bears much fruit [harvest]; for without Me you can do nothing . . . If you abide in Me, you will ask what you desire, and it shall be done for you. By this My Father is glorified, that you bear much fruit; so you will be My disciples. As the Father loved Me, I also have loved you; abide in My love. If you keep My commandments, you will abide in My love, just as I have kept My Father's commandments and abide in His love. These thing I have spoken to you, that My joy may remain in you, and that your joy may be full. This is My commandment, that you love one another as I have loved you. Greater love has no one than this, than to lay down one's life for his friends. You are My friends if you do whatever I command you" [John 15:5, 7-14, NKJV].

Prior to His ascension to be with His Father, Jesus also promised His disciples: "If you love me, you will keep my commandments. And I will ask the Father, and He will give you another Helper to be with you forever, even the Spirit of truth, whom the world cannot receive, because it neither sees him nor knows him. You know him, for he dwells with you and will be in you. I will not leave you as orphans; I will come to you. Yet a little while and the world will see me no more, but you will see me. Because I live, you also will live. In that day you will know that I am in my Father, and you in me, and I in you. Whoever has my commandments and keeps them, he it is who loves me. And he who loves me will be loved by my Father, and I will love him and manifest myself to him" [John 14:15- 21, ESV].

Jesus continued to teach His friends how the Helper—"the spirit of truth"— would operate in faithful disciples who kept His commandments: "If anyone loves Me, he will keep My word; and My Father will love him, and We will come to him and make Our home with him. He who does not love Me does not keep My words; and the word which you hear is not Mine but the Father's who sent Me. These things I have spoken to you while being present with you. But the Helper, the Holy Spirit, whom [which] the Father will send in My name, He [it] will teach you all things, and bring to your remembrance all things that I said to you" [John14:23-26, NKJV].

"I still have many things to say to you," Jesus continued. "but you cannot bear them now. However, when He [it], the Spirit of truth, has come, He [it] will guide you into all truth: for He [it] will not speak on His [its] own authority, but whatever He [it] hears [from the Father or from Me] He [it] will speak [reveal]; and He [it] will tell you things to come. He [it] will glorify Me, for He [it] will take of what is Mine and declare it to you. All things that the Father has are Mine. Therefore I said that He [it] will take of Mine and declare it to you" [John 16:12-15, NKJV].

Herein is a marvelous truth: Jesus teaches His disciples *precisely how* the gift of holy spirit will work in them after they receive [into evidence] the baptism in the spirit. Indeed, He reveals to them that the holy spirit will operate in them *exactly* the way it operated in Him during His earthly ministry *in the power of the spirit:* "I can of Myself do nothing. As I hear [from the Father by means of the manifestations of the spirit] I judge; and My judgment is righteous because I do not seek My own will, but the will of the Father who sent Me" [John 5:30, NKJV]. Jesus says to His disciples that the gift of holy spirit—"the spirit of truth"—"the Helper"—*will not speak on its own authority,* "but whatever He hears [from the Father or from Himself] He will speak [that is to say, *reveal to the believer by means of the manifestations of word of knowledge, word of wisdom and the discerning of spirits*], and He will tell you things to come [manifested via the spirit in prophecy or inspired teaching]. He will glorify Me [by means of the manifestations of miracles and gifts of healing and occasional phenomena], for He will take of what is Mine ["the knowledge of the mystery of God, both of the Father and of Christ, in whom are hidden all the treasures of wisdom and knowledge"—Colossians 2:2b,3, NKJV] and declare it to you" [by means of the revelation manifestations of the spirit].

It must be noted here that in most versions of the Bible the gift of holy spirit is referred to as "He." This is not substantiated in the Greek text. Indeed, when the gift of God is referred to as "He," such as in the NKJV, ESV, and NIV, it lends much confusion to our understanding. Moreover, capitalization of the pronouns referring to the gift as "He," "Who," or "Whom" are the private interpretation of the translators and are not justified by the text. The Greek language assigns a gender to nouns. Because the word for "counselor"—*parakletos*—in the Greek is a masculine noun, translators have assumed that the gift of holy spirit is a "he." Alas, the word for "spirit"—*pneuma*—is neuter in the Greek, and in the Hebrew the word for "spirit" is feminine. Proper translation depends on the context. When "holy spirit" refers to God, a pronoun must be translated "He" and capitalized. However, when the context refers to God's *gift*, any pronoun must be translated "it" and not capitalized. It's clear from the Lord's explanation of how the gift would operate in His disciples that the gift is neuter. The gift of holy spirit is not a "person" living in the believer. It does not have a mind or a personality of its own. Jesus makes this clear when He says : "He [it] will not speak on His [its] own authority, but whatever He [it] hears He [it] will speak . . . ." The gift of God—holy spirit— is the unique and living spiritual creation of God in "Christ in you" *enabling* the believer to communicate spiritually with God who is t*he* Holy Spirit, and it is the means by which and through which we can enjoy intimacy—holy communion—with our Lord who saved us and teaches us the way to the Father. Ephesians 1:13 and 14 in the KJV version of the Bible says: "In whom ye also trusted, after that ye heard the word of truth, the gospel of your salvation: in whom also after that ye believed, ye were sealed with that holy Spirit of promise, Which [*not* Whom] is the earnest of our inheritance until the redemption of the purchased possession, unto the praise of his glory." This is a correct use of the pronoun referring to the gift of holy spirit.

Now the question arises: Are there specific commandments for the members of Christ's spiritual Body—His "new creations" [*kainos*—"fresh, unprecedented"]? Jesus' commandments recorded in the Gospels can be summarized in a single declaration and are applicable today: "Hear, O Israel, the Lord our God is one. And you shall love the Lord your God with all your heart [*kardia*-"center and seat of spiritual life"], with all your soul [*psyche*-"seat of the feelings, desires, affections"], with all your mind [*dianoia*-"way of thinking, understanding"], and with all your strength [*ischys*-"force, ability, might"]. This is the first commandment. And the second, like it [*homoios*-"resembling, corresponding"], is this: You shall love your neighbor as yourself. There is no other commandment greater than these" [Mark 12:29-31, NKJV]. In order for a believer to obey and fulfill these commandments of the Lord, he must become a true disciple [*mathetes*-"learner, student"]. Jesus says: "A disciple is not above his teacher, but everyone who is perfectly trained will be like his teacher" [Luke 6:40, NKJV]. Specifically, "the Lord's curriculum" revealed to us in Paul's letters, are the commandments for the members of His Body: ". . . do not be conformed to this world, but be transformed by the renewal of your mind" [Romans 12:2]; ". . . praying always with all prayer and supplication in the spirit" [Ephesians 6:18]; ". . . put off your old self, which belongs to your former manner of life and is corrupt through deceitful desires . . . and put on the new self, created after the likeness of God in true righteousness and holiness" [Ephesians 4:22,23]; and "take up the whole armor of God, that you may be able to withstand in the evil day, and having done all, to stand firm" [Ephesians 6:13]. By inspiration from the Lord, John writes: "Brethren, I write no new commandment to you, but an old commandment which you have had from the beginning. The old commandment is the word which you heard from the beginning" [1 John 2:7, NKJV.]. The Psalmist says: "I have stored up your word in my heart, that I might not sin against you" [Psalm 119:11]. King David prays: "Create in me a clean [*tahowr:* "pure; ethically and morally"] heart, O God . . ." [Psalm 51:10]. And Proverbs 4:23 reminds us: "Keep your heart with all diligence, for out of it spring the issues [*towtsa'ah-*"outgoings, source"] of life" [NKJV].

True discipleship compels a believer to practice these things consistently and perseveringly; otherwise he is just "whistling Dixie," which, according to the definition of the idiom, means that someone talks about things in a more positive way than the reality, which is what most Christians do. As James tells us: "But be doers of the word, and not hearers only, deceiving yourselves. For if anyone is a hearer of the word and not a doer, he is like a man observing his natural face in a mirror [that is, he sees himself in the word of God as God sees him]; for he observes himself [the truth of who he really is in Christ], goes away, and immediately forgets what kind of man [God says] he was [because of his old nature and the cares of this world]. But he who looks [*parakypto-*"looks carefully into, inspects to the end of becoming acquainted with"] into the perfect law of liberty [of who we are in Christ] and continues in it, and is not a forgetful hearer but a doer of the work, this one will be blessed in what he does" [James 1:22-25, NKJV]. Fittingly, in His sermon on the plain, Jesus says: "Why do you call me 'Lord, Lord,' and not do what I tell you? Everyone who comes to me and hears my words and does them, I will show you what he is like: he is like a man building a house, who dug deep and laid the foundation on a rock. And when a flood arose, the stream broke against that house and could not shake it, because it had been well built. But the one who hears and does not do them is like a man who built a house on the ground without a foundation. When the stream broke against it, immediately it fell, and the ruin of that house was great" [Luke 6:46-49, ESV].

The Bible tells us that when God baptized His Son with holy spirit following His baptism in the Jordan by John, it was not by "measure," as He put the spirit on the prophets and a few others up until that time. The AMP says: "For since He Whom God has sent speaks the words of God (proclaims God's own message), God does not give Him His Spirit sparingly or by measure, but boundless is the gift God makes of His

Spirit" [John 3:34]. Thus Jesus could proclaim with all conviction in the synagogue in Nazareth: "The Spirit of the Lord is upon Me, because He has anointed Me to preach the gospel to the poor; He has sent Me to heal the brokenhearted, to proclaim liberty to the captives, and recovery of sight to the blind, to set at liberty those who are oppressed, to proclaim the acceptable year of the Lord" [Luke 4:18,18, NKJV].

In Old Testament times, God put His spirit by measure on a few people only, and the Scriptures tell us that the spirit was upon them conditionally, as long as they obeyed God. After Nathan the prophet confronted King David about his sin with Bathsheba, David implores God: "Create in me a clean heart, O God, and renew a steadfast spirit within me. Do not cast me away from Your presence, and do not take your Holy Spirit from me" [Psalm 51:10,11, NKJV].

"Born of God"

Everything changed at Pentecost. Pentecost ushered in a "new age" in God's timing—the administration or "dispensation of the grace of God" which, Paul says, "was given to me for you" [Gentiles] [Ephesians 3:2, NKJV]. Beginning at Pentecost the "rules" changed—the Mosaic Law was done with—fulfilled in Christ's sacrifice on the cross—and, with the baptism in holy spirit, believers in Jesus Christ were "born from above" for the first time: "Since you have purified your souls in obeying the truth through the Spirit in sincere love of the brethren, love one another fervently with a pure heart, having been born again [annagennao-"born anew, produced again, begat again"], not of corruptible seed [mortal], but incorruptible [spiritual] through the word of God which lives and abides forever" [1 Peter 1:23, NKJV]. Jesus told Nicodemus: "Most assuredly, I say to you, unless one is born again [gennao-"literally to be born, begotten"], he cannot see the kingdom of God . . . That which is born of the flesh is flesh, and that which is born of the Spirit is Spirit" [John 3:3,6, NKJV]. Jesus was talking about entering the kingdom of God [the Millennial Kingdom] after His return to this earth. However, the principle is the same for believers in this Age of God's Grace prior to the Lord's return, as John testifies in his first letter: "Whoever believes that Jesus is the Christ is born [gennao] of God, and everyone who loves Him who begot [gennao] also loves him who is begotten [gennao] of Him" [1 John 5:1, NKJV]. And: "If you know that He [Christ] is righteous, you know that everyone who practices righteousness is born [*gennao*] of Him" [1 John 2:29, NKJV]. Moreover, Ephesians 1:13,14 says: "In Him [Christ] you also trusted, after you heard the word of truth, the gospel of your salvation, in whom also, having believed, you were sealed [*sphragizo*-"marked, secured, authenticated"] with the Holy Spirit of promise, who [which] is the guarantee [*arrabon*-"earnest, pledge, down payment"] of our inheritance until the redemption of the purchased possession [all believers at the Rapture of the Church] to the praise of His glory" [Ephesians 1:13,14, NKJV]. Since Pentecost believers in Jesus Christ are born anew spiritually—"new creations"—and sealed with the gift of holy spirit as a guarantee of all the "exceeding great and precious promises" of God [2 Peter 1:4] to His spiritually-begotten children [not everyone is a child of God—only those begotten by Him], not only in this mortal life, but also in the everlasting life to come.

Some Bible teachers have suggested that this "guarantee"—translated "earnest," "pledge," or "deposit" in various versions of the Bible—with which believers are "sealed" is merely a measure or a token of the fullness of the spirit God gave to His Son, even as it was during Old Testament times. Certainly few Christian believers down through the centuries have manifested even a semblance of the spiritual power and authority that Jesus Christ demonstrated during His earthly ministry. In the Greek text the word *arrabon*—translated "guarantee" in the NKJV and ESV, "deposit" in the NIV, "pledge" in the NASB, and "earnest" in the YLT and Darby translations—refers to a guarantee of the "fullness" which believers will receive at the judgment seat of Christ following the Rapture of the Church when "we shall be like Him [transformed into His glorious likeness] for we shall see Him as He is" [1 John 3:2b, NKJV]. However, it does not imply that this "deposit" or "pledge" is somehow short of the full *potential* of "Christ in you." The Scriptures teach otherwise. Ephesians 1:22,23 says: "And He [God] put all things under His [Christ's] feet, and gave Him to be head over all things to the church, which is His body, the fullness [*pleroma*-"completeness"] of Him who fills [*pleroo*-"fills to the full, supplied liberally, abounding"] all in all" [NKJV]. And Colossians 2:9,10 tell us that "in Him [Christ] dwells all the fullness [*pleroma*] of the Godhead bodily; and you are complete [*pleroo*-"filled to the full, abounding"] in Him, who is the head of all principality and power" [NKJV]. As well, Ephesians 1:3 assures us that "God has blessed us with every spiritual blessing in the heavenly places in Christ" [NKJV]. If Christians are "complete in Him," then we cannot receive any more "completeness" than we already have until such time as we see Him "face to face" and become like Him. If God has blessed us with "every spiritual blessing in the heavenly places" already, then what more blessing do we need? And if Christians have only a "measure" or "token" of holy spirit like Old Testament believers had, then how could God say it is *"Christ in you . . ."*?

And so we are faced, once again, with a dilemma: Why do most Christian believers demonstrate so little of the spiritual power and authority Jesus promised? There are reasons. To begin, let us consider 2 Corinthians 5:17 which says: "Therefore, if anyone is in Christ, he is a new creation; old things have passed away; behold, all things have become new" [NKJV]. The ESV says: "The old has passed away; behold, the new has come." Indeed!—the "new has come"—*but not yet fully mature.* Paul writes to the Galatian believers: "My little children, for whom I labor in birth again until Christ is formed in you, I would like to be present with you now and to change my tone; for I have doubts about you" [Galatians 4:19,20, NKJV]. Christ *formed* in a believer is a process. Few Christians commit their lives to learning to love the Lord our God "with all your heart, with all your soul, with all your mind, and with all your strength." This is not to say that down through the centuries certain believers have demonstrated dramatically aspects of Christ's authority in prophecy, the working of miracles, or gifts of healing. And yet the promise of John 14:12 is to every member of the Body of Christ.

Not understanding how God designed the gift of holy spirit to work in them, and that it takes knowledge, dedication and faithfulness in order to grow in grace, many Christians hope that from time to time God will "give them a handout." God won't do it. "Not that we are sufficient of ourselves to think of anything as being from ourselves," Paul says to the Corinthians, "but our sufficiency is from God" [2 Corinthians 3:5, NKJV]. In the Greek text the word for "sufficiency" is *hikanotes*, meaning "ability, competency." In 2 Corinthians 9:8, in regard to sowing and reaping, he says: "And God is able to make all grace abound toward you, that you, always having all sufficiency in all things, may have an abundance for every good work" [NKJV]. In the Greek the word for "sufficiency" here is *autarkeia*, which means "overflowing, exceeding, redounding." And in this same verse "make," "abound," and "abundance" are all one word in the Greek—*perisseuo*, meaning "a perfect condition in which no aid or support is needed." And in 2 Corinthians 12, when Paul pleads with the Lord three times that the "thorn in the flesh" might depart from him, the Lord says: "My grace is sufficient [*arkeo*-"possessed of unfailing strength"] for you, for My strength is made perfect in weakness" [NKJV]. Jesus reminds Paul that the *dunamis* of "Christ in you" is more than enough for him to deal with the situation. Therefore, Paul says in Philippians 4:13: "I can do all things through Christ who strengthens me" [NKJV]. And this is an important key for our understanding—God doesn't give handouts—He has *already enabled us* to deal with life's challenging situations if we will learn to walk by the spirit in faith that "God is our sufficiency." It's enlightening to understand, for example, that some believers fail to manifest the spirit—speak in tongues—even after they have been taught that "Jesus said I could and Paul said I should"—because they expect God to *cause* them to speak. God won't do it. God has already acted—He *enabled* us to manifest the spirit but we must do the speaking. Fittingly, the word *lambano* means "receive into evidence" or, in a fuller sense, "to lay hold of . . . in order to use it." Every believer has been enabled with *dunamis*, but if he doesn't "lay hold of" and actively receive the blessing, it won't happen.

Another reason for "spiritual impotence" within the Body of Christ can be learned from Peter's warning to "the pilgrims of the Dispersion" [1 Peter 1:1]: "Beloved, I beg you as sojourners and pilgrims, abstain from fleshly lusts which war against the soul" [1 Peter 2:11,NKJV], which corresponds with Paul's warning to believers in Galatians 5:16,17: "I say then, walk in the Spirit, and you shall not fulfill the lust [*epithymia*-"craving, desire for what is forbidden"] of the flesh. For the flesh lusts against the Spirit, and the Spirit against the flesh, and these are contrary to one another, so that you do not do the things that you wish" [NKJV]. This is a trap and a failure for many Christians, even pastors and other leaders in the Church.

The demonstration of the power and authority of "Christ in you" demands genuine faith in the promises of God, not mere mental assent. As well, it demands doing the will of the Lord, as Jesus did, not preferring one's own will. In Matthew 17:20 and in Mark 11:23 Jesus teaches His disciples: "Have faith in [or, "have the faith of"] God. Truly, I say to you, whoever says to this mountain, 'Be taken up and thrown into the sea,' and does not doubt in his heart, but believes that what he says will come to pass, it will be done for him. Therefore I tell you, whatever you ask in prayer, believe that you have received it, and it will be yours. And whenever you stand praying, forgive, if you have anything against anyone, so that your Father also who is in heaven may forgive you your trespasses" [ESV], [just as Jesus prayed on the cross: "Father, forgive them, for they know not what they do"—Luke 23:34, ESV]. Jesus says the "mountain" will be "taken up and thrown into the sea" if the one speaking "does not doubt in his heart, but believes that what he says will come to pass." But how is it possible to arrive at the place in our heart where we are not doubting at all? There are only two possibilities: persevering in prayer and waiting on the Lord if the situation is not urgent, or the operation of the manifestation of believing faith as the result of a word of knowledge and a word of wisdom from the Lord.

Prayers are answered and "mountains" can be "moved" over time by persistent prayer [Jesus says "don't quit."] and steadfast faith—"Wait on the Lord; be of good courage, and He shall strengthen your heart; wait, I say, on the Lord" [Psalm 27:14, NKJV]. The only revelation required in such an instance is the word of God because God's word is revelation. In Acts 12 when Peter was seized and put in prison, "earnest prayer was made to God for him by the church . . . Now when Herod was about to bring him out, on that very night, Peter was sleeping between two soldiers, bound with two chains, and sentries before the door were guarding the prison. And behold, an angel of the Lord stood next to him [phenomenon], and a light shone in the cell. He struck Peter on the side and woke him, saying, 'Get up quickly.' And the chains fell off his hands [miracle, phenomenon]. And the angel said to him, 'Dress yourself and put on your sandals.' And he did so. And he said to him, 'Wrap your cloak around you and follow me.' And he went out and followed him. He did not know that what was being done by the angel was real, but thought he was seeing a vision. When they had passed the first and the second guard, they came to the iron gate leading into the city. It opened for them of its own accord [miracle, phenomenon], and they went out and went along one street, and immediately the angel left him. When Peter came to himself, he said, 'Now I am sure that the Lord has sent his angel and rescued me from the hand of Herod and from all that the Jewish people were expecting.' When he realized this, he went to the house of Mary, the mother of John whose other name was Mark, where many were gathered together and were praying" [Acts 12:4-12, ESV]. James 5:16 says: "The earnest (heartfelt, continued) prayer of a righteous man [as well as the whole church!] makes tremendous power available (dynamic in its working)" [AMP]. As well, Hebrews 13:2 reminds us: "Do not neglect to show hospitality to strangers, for thereby some have entertained angels unawares" [ESV].

In situations of urgency, however, we need direct revelation from the Lord by means of a word of knowledge and a word of wisdom. The Lord Jesus Christ is the head of the Body and we are the members. The Lord supplies the wisdom— what to do with the information He will give us— that we cannot know by our senses. James says: "If any of you lacks wisdom, let him ask of God, who gives to all liberally and without reproach, and it will be given to him. But let him ask in faith, with no doubting, for he who doubts is like a wave of the sea driven and tossed by the wind. For let not that man suppose that he will receive anything [knowledge and wisdom] from the Lord; he is a double-minded man, unstable in all his ways" [James 1:5-7, NKJV]. Few Christians understand that when Jesus says "whoever says to this mountain, 'Be taken up and thrown into the sea, and does not doubt in his heart . . . ,' He is saying that if a believer will act in *absolute believing faith* according to what He tells the believer to do by means of a word of knowledge and a word of wisdom, "it will be done for him." An instantaneous gift of healing or a miracle is a *manifestation* of the spirit *as the result* of a word of knowledge and a word of wisdom from the Lord and *acted on* in believing faith.

Some churches teach that all a believer has to do is to "speak to the mountain" and it will move immediately or eventually. That is naïve at best. Occasionally we read or hear in the media reports of Christian parents who, meaning well but deceived, pray for the Lord to heal their desperately ill child but have no understanding of the spiritual process—the Lord's protocol—and refuse to let medical professionals help, insisting that their "blind" faith will prevail. And when the child dies, everyone is shocked and saddened—and Christian "faith healing" is once again maligned in the media [the devil's playground]. Certainly the parents and others may pray intensely for the Lord to heal. And no doubt the Lord supplies knowledge and wisdom. But in such a case, are the parents *listening* for the Lord's guidance, or is their mind-set so contrary to medical help *despite* the Lord's guidance that they miss the revelation? In such a case their determination to rely only on the Lord's miraculous touch is simply misplaced humility. Doctors heal. Nurses heal. Why should believers think that the Lord cannot work in doctors and nurses to heal, and that somehow their faith is a failure if they turn to medicine for help?

"Ask, and it will be given"

However, let us not underestimate the grace and mercy of God. Our Father loves His children and sometimes heals and delivers in spite of our shortcomings. Jesus teaches that it is important to "Ask [and keep on asking], and it will be given to you; seek [and keep on seeking], and you will find; knock [and keep on knocking] and it will be opened to you. For everyone who asks [persistently] receives, and he who seeks [persistently] finds, and to him who knocks [persistently] it will be opened" [Luke 11:9, 10, NKJV]. As well, ". . . men ought always to pray and not lose heart" ["faint, give up, turn coward"—AMP]. Much of the time we simply don't know and do not understand the spiritual challenges "behind the scenes" of our senses knowledge. A record in Daniel 10 provides great insight: "In the third year of Cyrus King of Persia a message was revealed to Daniel, whose name was Belteshazzar; the message was true, but the appointed time was long, and he understood the message, and had understanding of the vision. In those days I, Daniel, was mourning three full weeks [because he understood Israel's terrible future]. I ate no pleasant food, no meat or wine came into my mouth, nor did I anoint myself at all, till three whole weeks were fulfilled. Now on the twenty-fourth day of the first month, as I was by the side of the great river, the Tigris, I lifted my eyes and looked, and behold, a certain man clothed in linen, whose waist was girded with gold of Uphaz!" [Daniel 10:1-5, NKJV].

The man who Daniel sees in a vision [word of knowledge, word of wisdom] is the archangel Gabriel, God's chief messenger. Daniel is astonished and overwhelmed by his glory so that "I was in a deep sleep on my face, with my face to the ground. Suddenly a hand touched me, which made me tremble on my knees and on the palms of my hands. And he said to me, 'O Daniel, man greatly beloved, understand the words that I speak to you and stand upright, for I have now been sent to you.' While he was speaking this word to me, I stood trembling.

Then he said to me, 'Do not fear, Daniel, for from the first day that you set your heart to understand and to humble yourself before your God, your words were heard; and I have come because of your words. But the prince [a major demon spirit] of the kingdom of Persia withstood me twenty-one days, and behold, Michael, one of the chief princes [the archangel who fights for God's people], came to help me, for I had been left alone there with the kings of Persia. Now I have come to make you understand what will happen to your people in the latter days, for the vision refers to many days yet to come" [vss. 9b-14, NKJV].

It's important to understand in this record that "from the first day that you set your heart to understand, and to humble yourself before your God, your words were heard" [by the Father]. God always hears our words as we pray. Yet it is clear from this record that spiritual realities "behind the scenes" of our knowing and understanding can delay God's response to our prayers. And that's why persistence and patience in prayer is so important. In all of our prayers of faith, our Father responds: "O child, greatly beloved . . . ," just as He responded to Daniel. Because of Christ's sacrifice on the cross of infamy and the gift of holy spirit poured out on all who confess His name, we are "qualified . . . to share in the inheritance of the saints in light" [Colossians 1:12], "delivered . . . from the power of the darkness of this world" [v. 13[, presented "holy, and blameless, and above reproach in His sight; and accepted in the Beloved" [Ephesians 1:6]; so that "there is therefore now no condemnation to those who are in Christ Jesus" [Romans 8:1]. "For He [God] made Him [Jesus] who knew no sin to be sin for us, that we might become the righteousness of God in Him" [2 Corinthians 5:21]; "Therefore, if anyone is in Christ he is a new [kainos-"new in quality, fresh, unprecedented"] creation" [v. 17], and we "are complete [pleroo-"filled to the full"] in Him, who is the head of all principality and power" [Colossians 2:10]; for "In Him you were also circumcised with the circumcision made without hands . . . buried with Him in baptism . . . raised with Him through faith in the working of God, who raised Him from the dead . . . made alive together with Him, having forgiven you all trespasses" [vss. 11-13]; so that we "have an anointing from the Holy One . . . ," and "the anointing which you have received from Him abides in you" [permanently] [1 John 2:20,27]; "For as many as are led by the Spirit of God, these are the sons of God . . . The Spirit Himself [God] bears witness with our Spirit [the gift] that we are children of

God, and if children, then heirs—heirs of God and joint heirs with Christ" [Romans 8:14-17]; which means, indeed, that "God has blessed us with every spiritual blessing in the heavenly places in Christ" [Ephesians 1:3]; so that God does not see us in our old nature but as "Christ in you, the hope of glory" [Colossians 1:27]; so that we may boldly say, as Paul declares in Galatians 2:20: "I have been crucified with Christ; it is no longer I who live, but Christ lives in me; and the life which I now live in the flesh I live by faith in the Son of God, who loved me and gave Himself for me."

As incredibly wonderful as the truth is, God reminds us "we have this treasure in earthen vessels that the excellence of the power [*dunamis*] may be of God and not of us" [2 Corinthians 4:7, NKJV]. And this is a paradox—the "yin and yang," the contrary forces of darkness and light, of the old nature and new nature, in our mortal beings. And this is precisely why our Lord has prescribed a "curriculum" of study and practice for those members of His Body who are determined to become like Him.

"No man is an island"

"No man is an island entire of itself; every man is a piece of the continent, a part of the main . . . ," the poet John Donne wrote, suggesting that people are not isolated from one another, but that mankind is interconnected. The Bible validates this truth, especially for the members of the Body of Christ: "For in one Spirit we were all baptized into one body—Jews or Greeks, slaves or free—and all were made to drink of one Spirit . . . For the body does not consist of one member but many . . . But God has so composed the body, giving greater honor to the part that lacked it, that there may be no division in the body, but that the members may have the same care for one another . . . Now you are the body of Christ and individually members of it" [1 Corinthians 12:13, 14, 24, 25, 27, ESV]. Moreover, Paul informs us in Ephesians 2:21,22 that "the whole [spiritual] building, being fitted together, grows into a holy temple in the Lord, in whom you also are being built together for a dwelling place of God in [or by] the Spirit" [NKJV].

No disciple of the Lord, no matter how knowledgeable or how determined, can accomplish very much on his own without the persistent prayers and unity in the spirit of the local Body of Christ of which he is a part. Acts 4 provides an important lesson on the effects of spiritual unity: "Now the multitude of those who believed were of one heart and one soul . . . And with great power the apostles gave witness to the resurrection of the Lord Jesus. And great grace [*charis*-"divine favor"] was upon them all" [4:32a, 33, NKJV]. Great unity of the spirit prevailed in this congregation of believers, great unity of purpose, and great love for the living presence of the Lord and for one another, and great faith in the leadership in the Church. As the result, God was able to work wonders among them by means of the abundance and clarity of the manifestations of holy spirit. This is the way God intended it to work in every fellowship of believers. But it must be understood that there has to be clarity of doctrine according to the accuracy of God's word so that there are no divisions, no factions in the group with each member holding to whatever religious tradition or theological point of view he chooses—for that is the recipe for a spiritually impotent church. Paul says to the Corinthians: "Now I plead with you, brethren, by the name of our Lord Jesus Christ, that you all speak the same thing, and that there be no divisions among you, but that you be perfectly joined together in the same mind and in the same judgment" [1 Corinthians 1:10, NKJV]. Again we are reminded of Paul's exhortation to Timothy: "As I urged you when I went into Macedonia—remain in Ephesus that you may charge some that they teach no other doctrine . . ." [1 Timothy 1:3, NKJV]; "If you instruct the brethren in these things, you will be a good minister of Jesus Christ, nourished in the words of faith and of the good doctrine which you have carefully followed" [1 Timothy 4:6, NKJV]; "Take heed to yourself and to the doctrine. Continue in them, for in doing this you will save both yourself and those who hear you" [4:16]. What doctrine is Paul talking about?—the doctrine the Lord gave to him by revelation [Galatians 1] —this is "the Lord's curriculum." For churches that fail to teach "the Lord's curriculum," His judgment applies: "This people honors me with their lips, but their heart is far from me; in vain do they worship me, teaching as doctrines the commandments of men. You leave the commandment of God and hold to the tradition of men" [Mark 7:6-8, ESV]. Alas, in most of our churches, and even in independent Pentecostal groups, believers have been taught much doctrinal error that leads to the defeat of the promises of God. The truth is, there is a spiritual damper on wrong doctrine. Faith in wrong doctrine is faith that is bankrupt.

The "one heart and one soul" record in Acts 4 also implies a "phenomenon of the family faith" in a fellowship of believers where there is great unity of purpose, inspired teaching, preaching and exhortation, and often uplifting music in praise and worship. In Acts 4 all the believers loved the Lord "with all their heart, and with all their soul, and with all their mind, and with all their strength"—and at that time, loved their neighbors as themselves! In a spiritual sense, they "*stepped out of themselves and into Him.*" Participants in such a gathering today often experience a sense of the living presence of the Lord accompanied by a dynamic "wave of faith" sweeping over the place where they are gathered, which lends itself to the manifestations of the spirit in operation freely, especially with the laying on of hands for prayer and the ministering of healing. In such an atmosphere of faith and expectation, captives are set free.

Such "one heart and one soul" happenings are infrequent in the Church today. It's not because the Lord is miserly in benevolence. It's because there is so little faith. Spiritually mature leaders in the Church need to understand that in order to "walk in His steps," we need to *practice, practice, practice.* John says: "If you know that He is righteous, you know that everyone who practices [*poieo*-"produce, construct, cause, prepare"] righteousness is born of Him" [1 John 2:29, NKJV]. It is *necessary* to *practice* righteous living in order to get good at it, including operating the manifestations of the spirit on behalf of the Body. At every opportunity for intercessory prayer, or for the laying on of hands for the ministering of healing to those in need, we must not hesitate to join in. Paul wrote to his timid protégé Timothy: "For God has not given us a spirit of fear [timidity], but of power [*dunamis*] and of love [*agape*] and of a sound [disciplined] mind" [2 Timothy 1:7, NKJV]. And he says in Hebrews: "Let us therefore come boldly [with confidence] to the throne of grace, that we may obtain mercy and find grace to help in time of need" [4:16, NKJV]. As Jesus proved to us in His earthly ministry, God is righteous to intervene at every opportunity and in every instance to strengthen and deliver His children according to our believing faith and persistence in prayer. We don't need to wait on the Lord for a "go signal" in order to pray or minister to someone's need. Too often needs are not met because even mature believers think they need to wait on God to give them a word of knowledge and a word of wisdom rather than acting on what He has already done for us. God has already assured us it is "Christ in you." We are enabled. We have the *dunamis* and the *exousia* in the name of Jesus Christ. *As we act in faith*, He supplies the guidance to handle the situation. In other words: Unreservedly embrace every opportunity to "set the captives free."

"Walk in love"

"A new commandment I give to you," Jesus said to His disciples prior to His passion, "that you love [*agape*] one another; as I have loved you, that you also love one another. By this all will know that you are My disciples, if you have love for one another" [John 13:34,35, NKJV]. "As the Father loved Me, I also have loved you; abide in My love. If you keep My commandments, you will abide in My love, just as I have kept My Father's commandments and abide in His love. These things I have spoken to you, that My joy may remain in you, and that your joy may be full. This is My commandment, that you love one another as I have loved you . . . You did not choose Me, but I chose you and appointed you that you should go and bear fruit, and that your fruit should remain, that whatever you ask the Father in My name, He may give you. These things I command you, that you love one another" [John 15:9-12, 16, 17, NKJV]. "And above all things," Peter writes, "have fervent love for one another, for love will cover a multitude of sins" [1 Peter 4:8, NKJV]. And Paul says: "Though I speak with the tongues of men and of angels, and have not love, I have become sounding brass or a clanging cymbal. And though I have ["the gift of" is not in the Greek] prophecy and understand all mysteries and all knowledge, and though I have all faith, so that I could remove mountains, but have not love, I am nothing . . . and now abide faith, hope, love, these three; but the greatest of these is love" [1 Corinthians 13:1, 2, 13, NKJV].

It is difficult, perhaps impossible, to practice the love of God to the extent of loving one's neighbor as one's self and obeying the Lord's commandment to "love your enemies, bless those who curse you, do good to those who hate you, and pray for those who spitefully use you and persecute you, that you may be sons of your Father in heaven" [Matthew 5:44, 45a, NKJV] unless one is progressing dynamically in "the Lord's curriculum." Fortunately "the steps of a good man are ordered by the Lord, and He delights in his way. Though he fall, he shall not be utterly cast down; for the Lord upholds him with His hand" [Psalm 37:23,24, NKJV]; "The Lord is gracious and full of compassion, slow to anger and great in mercy" [Psalm 145:8, NKJV]; "For the Lord is good; His mercy is everlasting, and His truth endures to all generations" [Psalm 100:5, NKJV]; "He is rich in mercy" [Ephesians 2:4], and "the Father of mercies and God of all comfort, who comforts us in all our tribulation [*thlipsis*-"pressure, affliction, distress, straits"], that we may be able to comfort those who are in trouble, with the comfort by which we ourselves are comforted by God" [2 Corinthians 1:3,4, NKJV].

Matthew tells us in his gospel that after Jesus cured a child who had a demon, His disciples came to Him and asked, "'Why could we not cast it out?' So Jesus said to them, 'Because of your unbelief; for assuredly, I say to you, if you have faith as a mustard seed, you will say to this mountain, 'Move from here to there,' and it will move; and nothing will be impossible for you'" [Matthew 17:19,20, NKJV]. He said: "Nothing will be impossible for you." *Nothing.*

Conclusion

Our Heavenly Father wants His children to be knowledgeable and wise concerning "the things of the spirit." He has, therefore, provided us with spiritual truths and practical keys so that, as we progress, we may become "conformed to the image of His Son." These truths and keys include: "I am the Lord who heals you;" that believers today are "born from above," "sealed with the Holy Spirit of promise," and clothed with "power from on high," which is the "anointing" of "Christ in you, the hope of glory." Moreover, He has provided us with a curriculum of study and practice which includes the renewal of our minds to the word of God, perseverance in prayer, putting off the old self and putting on the new, as well as putting on "the whole armor of God." In His word, God teaches us how to "walk by the spirit," which is to "walk by faith," which is to "imitate God" as beloved children and walk in love. Moreover, He has provided us with an abundance of teachable examples of how Jesus "set the captives free" "in the power of the spirit," and how His disciples did it by means of the manifestations of the spirit. And He encourages every one of us "to grow up into Him who is the head" so that we may do the works that He did: "Heal the brokenhearted, proclaim liberty to the captives and recovery of sight to the blind, and to set at liberty those who are oppressed." May our hearts proclaim: "Now thanks be to God who always leads us in triumph in Christ, and through us diffuses the fragrance of His knowledge in every place" [2 Corinthians 2:14, NKJV].

In his letter to the Ephesians, Paul prays "that the God of our Lord Jesus Christ, the Father of glory, may give to you the spirit of wisdom and revelation in the knowledge of Him, the eyes of your understanding being enlightened . . ." [1:17, 18a, NKJV]. Believers in Jesus Christ are on a spiritual journey of enlightenment. The Truth dawns on us. It is progressive. The more we step into God's living word, the deeper and richer it becomes. Finally, Paul says: "Brothers, I do not consider that I have made it my own. But one thing I do: forgetting what lies behind and straining forward to what lies ahead, I press on toward the goal of the prize of the upward call of God in Christ Jesus. Let those of us who are mature think this way, and if in anything you think otherwise, God will reveal that also to you. Only let us hold true to what we have attained" [Philippians 3:13-16, ESV].

The secret to holy spirit authority? "Out of me, Lord, and into You."

Summary
How can believers do it today?

Continue in "the Lord's curriculum." Abide in Him. Holy spirit operates in believers today in exactly the way it operated in Jesus and in His disciples in the early Church. Believers today are spiritually enabled to deal effectively with life's challenges if we will learn to walk by the spirit in faith that "God is our sufficiency." "No man is an island:" We are all members of Christ's Body. Love one another, as Christ loves us. "If you have faith as a mustard seed . . . nothing will be impossible for you." *Nothing.*

Verse to Remember: "I have strength for all things in Christ Who empowers me [I am ready for anything and equal to anything through Him Who infuses inner strength into me;] I am self-sufficient in Christ's sufficiency" [Philippians 4:13, AMP].

Question to ask Myself: Do people see in me that I have "been with Jesus"?

Exercise: Thank the Lord for guiding you in the way He would have you go. Paul says: "Having gifts that differ according to the grace given to us, let us use them: if prophecy, in proportion to our faith; if service, in our serving; the one who teaches, in his teaching; the one who exhorts, in his exhortation; the one who contributes, in generosity; the one who leads, with zeal; the one who does acts of mercy, with cheerfulness" [Romans 12:6-8, ESV]. If your ministry is that of a prayer warrior for others, practice it. If your faith is to be more proactive, then in your fellowship group, as you are inspired by the spirit, ask if anyone needs prayer for healing or for guidance from the Lord. When appropriate, lay your hands on them, thanking the Lord for a message of knowledge, a message of wisdom, the discerning of spirits, and for the Lord to energize the *dunamis* in you for the working of a miracle or a gift of healing in His name. Practice this. Take every opportunity to step out in faith. That means *out of your comfort zone.* "For God has not given us a spirit of fear, but of power and of love and of a sound mind" [2 Timothy 1:7, ESV].

POSTSCRIPT

**"He existed before anything else,
and He holds all things together"
[Colossians 1:17, NLT]**

"The heavens declare the glory of God; and the firmament shows His handiwork. Day unto day utters speech, and night unto night reveals knowledge" [Psalm 19:1, NKJV].

Astronomers have been perplexed for years with observations by the Hubble Space Telescope of very distant supernovae that showed that, a long time ago, the Universe was actually expanding more slowly than it is today. The expansion of the Universe has not been slowing due to the attractive force of gravity, as they once thought; rather, it has been accelerating. "No one expected this," NASA Science reports. "No one knew how to explain it. But something was causing it." Moreover, no one understood why the galaxies held together, even as the Universe expanded. For example, how does a spiral galaxy like the Milky Way maintain its spiral and not flail itself out into deep space since, scientists determined, gravity alone is not strong enough to hold the billions of spiraling stars in place? Recently they've discovered the mysterious existence of what they are calling "dark matter" and "dark energy"—"dark" because they can't see it or analyze it scientifically. Some scientists call this dark mystery "quintessence" which, they speculate, is causing the billions of galaxies throughout the Universe to cohere and not destroy themselves.

As well, scientists say they believe normal matter—the earth and everything on it, the planets, the stars, comets, etc.—constitutes less than 5% of the entire Universe. "Dark matter," they say, makes up about 25% of the Universe, and "dark energy" the remaining 70%. This "quintessence" of "dark matter" and "dark energy" is what the Science Channel (SCI) calls "the missing Universe." They say "an enormous chunk of the Universe seems to be invisible," and that "dark energy" is "the unknown variable in our quest to crack the cosmic code."

The Bible has something to say about this "quintessence"—this "invisible Universe:" "For it was in Him [God] that all things were created, in heaven and on earth, things seen and things unseen, whether thrones, dominions, rulers, or authorities; all things were created and exist through Him (by His service, intervention) and in and for Him. And He Himself existed before all things, and in Him all things consist (cohere, are held together)" [Colossians 1:16,17, AMP]. Other versions of the Bible read "hold together." In the Greek, this is the word *synistemi* meaning, according to Strong's Lexicon, "to bring or band together, introduce, put together by way of composition, teach, show, exhibit."

Could it be that this "quintessence"—this "invisible Universe"—is the Spirit of the Living God—we might call the *Breath of Holiness*—causing "all things [the whole Universe] to consist [and] cohere"? John 4:24 informs us that "God is Spirit, and those who worship Him must worship in spirit and truth" [NKJV]. God is Spirit [*pneuma*] and He is holy [*hagion*]. God is Holy Spirit—*pneuma hagion*—and He is invisible: "No one has seen God at any time" [1 John 4:12].

Genesis 1:27 informs us that "God created man in His own image ["God is Spirit"]; in the image of God He created him;" and then verse 2:7 says that "the Lord God formed man of the dust of the ground, and breathed [figure of speech: *anthropopatheia*] into his nostrils the breath of life; and man became a living being" [NKJV]. In the beginning man was a three-part being—body, soul, and spirit. Isaiah 43:7: "Everyone who is called by My name, whom I have created [*bara*-"create (always with God as subject)" = spirit] for My glory; I have formed him [*yatsar*-"fashion, frame" = body], yes, I have made him" [*asah*-"accomplish, act, effect" = soul] [NKJV]. "And the Lord God commanded the man, saying, 'Of every tree of the garden you may freely eat; but of the tree of the knowledge of good and evil you shall not eat, for in the day [*the very day*] that you eat of it you shall surely die'" [Genesis 2:16,17, NKJV]. Alas, when Adam and Eve committed treason against God in their disobedience, something about them died that very day—the spirit that God created in the man and woman, enabling them to commune spiritually with their Creator and to receive knowledge and wisdom beyond their five senses. When the spirit of God in them died, each became a two-part being of body and soul—no longer able to receive and to discern spiritual information from God: "The person without the Spirit ["natural man"—NKJV] does not accept the things that come from the Spirit of God but considers them foolishness and cannot understand them, because they are discerned only through the Spirit" [1 Corinthians 2:14, NIV]. This is the very state of "natural man" today: "always learning [by means of the five senses] and never able to arrive at a knowledge of the truth" [2 Timothy 3:7, ESV].

Our Heavenly Father's purpose and plan concerning His Son, Jesus Christ, was for the redemption of humanity from their fallen state by their being born of His spirit: "For God so loved the world that He gave His only begotten Son that whoever believes in Him should not perish but have everlasting life" [John 3:16, NKJV]. For a person to have everlasting life, he must be "born of God" [1 John 5:1]. Indeed 1 Peter says: ". . . love one another fervently with a pure heart, having been born again, not of corruptible seed but incorruptible, through the word of God which lives and abides forever" [1:22,23, NKJV]. And this living word through which we have been "born again" is *theopneustos*—"God breathed" [2 Timothy 3:16].

Following His resurrection, Jesus appeared to His disciples and said to them: "'Peace to you! As the Father has sent Me, I also send you.' And when He had said this, He breathed on *them*, and said to them, 'Receive [*lambano*] the Holy Spirit'" [John 20:21.22, NKJV]. In the NKJV, *them* is in italics, indicating that the word is not in the Greek text. It is incorrectly supplied in the English. The word for "breathed" is *emphysao* meaning "to breathe or to blow." Strong's Lexicon says: "The Greek word here is employed nowhere else in the New Testament, but is the very one used by the Septuagint translators of Genesis 2:7: 'And the Lord God formed man of the dust of the ground and *breathed* into his nostrils the breath of life; and man became a living soul.'" In this record in John 20:22, Jesus is *not* imparting holy spirit to His disciples, contrary to the teaching of some. He is merely instructing them *how to receive into evidence* the gift of holy spirit when it would become available at Pentecost. Jesus did not breath "on *them*." He simply breathed inwardly, showing His disciples how to react to the phenomena of the "sound from heaven" and the "tongues, as of fire."

"When the Day of Pentecost had fully come . . ." [Acts 2:1a, NKJV]. The Day of Pentecost had been in the process of arriving for thousands of years—since the very day the spirit of God in Adam and Eve died.

"And suddenly there came a sound from heaven, as of a rushing mighty wind, and it filled [*pleroo*-"to capacity"] the whole house where they were sitting" [Acts 2:2, NKJV]. The Greek words for "rushing mighty wind" are *phero biaios pnoe*. *Phero* means "to carry, gust, rush" or "moved inwardly, prompted." *Pnoe* means "breath, breath of life, wind." This verse can more accurately be translated: "And suddenly there came a sound from heaven, as of a *heavy breathing* [italics supplied], and it filled the whole house where they were sitting. Then there appeared to them divided tongues, as of fire, and one sat upon each of them. And they were all filled [*pletho*-"filled to overflowing"] with the Holy Spirit and began to speak with other tongues, as the Spirit gave them utterance" [Acts 2:2-4, NKJV]. Indeed, this was in wondrous fulfillment of the Lord's prophetic instructions to His disciples.

On the Day of Pentecost Peter, filled to overflowing with the spirit, raised his voice and said to the people: "This Jesus, God has raised up, of which we are all witnesses. Therefore being exalted to the right hand of God, and having received from the Father the promise of the Holy Spirit, He poured out this which you now see and hear" [Acts 2:32,33, NKJV]. Since Pentecost believers in Jesus Christ are "born from above" by the spirit of God which has been "poured out" by the Lord—the very *Breath of Holiness* that causes the whole Universe to consist and cohere! Thus believers in Jesus Christ are no longer "natural" men and women of body and soul, but "complete in Him"—"new creations" of body, soul, and spirit. Therefore Paul writes to the Thessalonians: "Now may the God of peace Himself sanctify you completely; and may your whole spirit, soul, and body be preserved blameless at the coming of our Lord Jesus Christ. He who calls you is faithful, who also will do it" [1 Thessalonians 5:23,24, NKJV].

*

A prayer: "One thing I have desired of the Lord, that will I seek: that I may dwell in the house [*bayith*-"dwelling, presence"] of the Lord all the days of my life, to behold the beauty of the Lord, and to inquire in His holy temple [*heykel*-"sanctuary"]. For in the time of trouble He shall hide me [*tsaphan*-"as treasure"] in His pavilion [*cok*-"covert, tabernacle"]: in the secret [*cether*-"shelter, covering"] of His tabernacle [*ohel*-"dwelling, habitation, presence"] shall He hide me; He shall set me upon a rock" [Psalm 27:4,5, NKJV].

"For the perverse person is an abomination to the Lord, but His secret counsel [*cowd*—"familiar converse, intimacy"] is with the upright" [Proverbs 3:32, NKJV].

"The secret [*cowd*] of the Lord is with those who fear Him, and He will show them His covenant [*beriyth*—"alliance, man-to-man pledge"]" [Psalm 25:14, NKJV].

About the Author

When I was twelve years old, I loved to listen to a Sunday evening radio broadcast entitled *The Master Speaks*. I'd lay in bed thinking about school the next day, and then the narrator would say, "Come with us to the hillsides of Galilee. The people have gathered there to hear The Master." And then he'd say, "Listen! The Master speaks." And I'd picture Jesus standing in the sunshine by the seaside speaking intriguing words, words that touched my heart: "I am the light of the world. He who follows Me shall not walk in darkness, but have the light of life." Sometimes it seemed like He was speaking to me face to face. It was on one of those Sunday evenings listening to The Master that I gave my heart to Him and confessed Him as my Lord and Savior. I was baptized in holy spirit at that time but, of course, I did not even know it.

Throughout high school occasionally I went with a friend to Bible classes at our local Baptist church, but I was mostly out of touch with Jesus until many years later. Those years of wandering and how I kept searching for "the Light" in all the wrong places before eventually coming back home to Him, in a spiritual sense, are chronicled in my first book, *The Hope of Glory: In Search of the Light*, published in 1979.

In September 1970, when I was twenty seven, while living in San Francisco, I was invited to take an intensive film class on keys to understanding the Bible. As the class unfolded, I felt ushered into the presence of the Lord by the gracious words that the teacher spoke, for "the word of God is living," the teacher said, "and powerful, and sharper than any two-edged sword, piercing even to the division of soul and spirit, and of joints and marrow, and is a discerner of the thoughts and intents of the heart." It was about halfway through the class, on perhaps the fifth or sixth evening, when it seemed that the teacher in the film pointed directly at me and said, "To you God willed to make known what are the riches of the glory of this mystery among the Gentiles: which is *Christ in you, Christ in you, Christ in YOU—the hope of glory!"* And as the teacher spoke those words, it was as if the spirit in my heart *burned with hunger*, and I knew at that moment that I had begun a hallowed quest to learn and to understand just what "Christ in you" was all about.

Days before I completed the Bible class, a friend from the class began telling me about the baptism in holy spirit and the manifestations of the spirit, especially speaking in tongues. I was eager to learn. As he demonstrated speaking in tongues for me, I asked him, "Can I do that?" He said, "Sure, if you want to," and then he taught me how. And so that evening I began speaking in tongues "the wonderful works of God."

It's been more than forty years since I began that quest to discover the fullness of "Christ in you." Over the years on several occasions I've manifested the reality in my own life that "by whose stripes you were healed" [1 Peter 2:24b, NKJV], and for years I've had the privilege of ministering healing and deliverance to others in prayer and with the laying on of hands. As well, I've experienced two miraculous epiphanies that changed my life and brought me closer to the Lord. Indeed I have "tasted that the Lord is gracious"[1 Peter 2:3, NKJV]. *The Secret to Holy Spirit Authority: In the Power of the Spirit* is the heart and unfolding of what I've learned from great teachers over these years and have personally discovered and experienced.

David Charles Craley
October 2011

BIBLIOGRAPHY

Bennett, Dennis J., *Nine O'Clock in the Morning,* Bridge-Logos Publishers, Alachua FL, 1970. Christian Educational Services, *Angelic Warfare,* www.TruthOrTradition.com, a division of Spirit & Truth International, Indianapolis IN.

_____*Prayer: Taking Hold of God's Willingness,* www.TruthOrTradition.com, a division of Spirit & Truth International, Indianapolis IN.

_____*The Armor of God—Stand!,* www.TruthOrTradition.com, a division of Spirit & Truth International, Indianapolis IN.

_____*The Power of Prayer,* www.TruthOrTradition.com, a division of Spirit & Truth International, Indianapolis IN.

_____*What does the Bible really say about healing?,* www.TruthOrTradition. com, a division of Spirit & Truth International, Indianapolis IN.

_____*What is Speaking in Tongues and why does God say to do it?* www. TruthOrTradition.com, a division of Spirit & Truth International, Indianapolis IN.

_____*What is The Key to Divine Intervention?,* www.TruthOrTradition. com, a division of Spirit & Truth International, Indianapolis IN.

_____*What is the point of prayer?,* www.TruthOrTradition.com, a division of Spirit & Truth International, Indianapolis IN.

Graeser, Mark H., John A. Lynn and John W. Schoenheit, *Don't Blame God!,* Christian Educational Services, Indianapolis IN, 1994.

_____*The Gift of Holy Spirit: The Power to Be Like Christ,* Christian Educational Services, Indianapolis IN, Third Edition, 2006.

Hagin, Kenneth E., *The Believer's Authority,* Rhema Bible Church, Tulsa OK, Legacy Edition, 2009.

Howard, Rick and Jamie Lash, *This Was Your Life! Preparing to Meet God Face to Face,* Chosen Books, a division of Baker Publishing Group, Grand Rapids MI, 1998.

Kenyon, E. W., *New Creation Realities,* Kenyon Gospel Publishing Society, Lynnwood WA, 1989.

_____*The Wonderful Name of Jesus,* Kenyon Gospel Publishing Society, Lynnwood WA, 1989.

_____*In His Presence,* Kenyon Gospel Publishing Society, Lynnwood WA, 1999.

_____*Jesus the Healer,* Kenyon Gospel Publishing Society, Lynnwood WA, 2004.

Sherrill, John L., *They Speak with Other Tongues,* Baker Book House, Grand Rapids MI, 1964.

Schoenheit, John W., *The Christian's Hope: The Anchor of the Soul,* Christian Educational Services, Indianapolis IN, 2001.

Warren, Rick, *The Purpose Driven Life,* Zondervan, Grand Rapids MI, 2002.

Wierwille, Victor Paul, *Power For Abundant Living,* American Christian Press, New Knoxville OH, 1971.

_____*The Bible Tells Me So,* American Christian Press, New Knoxville OH, 1971.

_____*The New, Dynamic Church,* American Christian Press, New Knoxville OH, 1971.

_____*Receiving the Holy Spirit Today,* American Christian Press, New Knoxville OH, 1972.

_____*The Word's Way,* American Christian Press, New Knoxville OH, 1971.

_____*God's Magnified Word,* American Christian Press, New Knoxville OH, 1977.

_____*Order My Steps In Thy Word,* American Christian Press, New Knoxville OH, 1985.